DIAMOND HEART
Book Two
The Freedom To Be

Other books by A.H. Almaas:

The Elixir of Enlightenment

Essence
The Diamond Approach to Inner Realization

Luminous Night's Journey
An Autobiographical Fragment

DIAMOND MIND SERIES
Volume I: **The Void**
Inner Spaciousness and Ego Structure

Volume II: **The Pearl Beyond Price**
*Integration of Personality into Being:
An Object Relations Approach*

Volume III: **The Point of Existence**
*Transformations of Narcissism
in Self-Realization*

DIAMOND HEART SERIES
Book One: **Elements of the Real in Man**
Book Three: **Being and the Meaning of Life**

DIAMOND HEART

Book Two

The Freedom To Be

A. H. Almaas

Diamond Books Berkeley, California

For the permission to reprint a poem, the author is grateful to the following:
White Pine Press for *The View from Cold Mountain—Poems of Han-shan and Shih-te*, translator Arthur Tobias, Copyright © 1982.

Cover photo: "The Wall of Peace" in Kuwait—photo and sculpture by Jafar Islah.

First published in 1989 by
Diamond Books
Almaas Publications
P.O. Box 10114
Berkeley, CA 94709

Second printing / March 1993
Third printing / June 1995
Fourth printing / October 1997

ISBN 0-936713-04-6

Library of Congress Card Catalog Number: 88–051949

Typeset in 11 point Galliard Roman by Byron Brown

Printed in the United States by BookCrafters

In my former days of bitter poverty
every night I counted other people's wealth
today I thought and thought then thought it through
everyone really must make their own
I dug and found a hidden treasure
a crystal pearl completely pure
even if that blue-eyed foreigner of great ability
wanted to buy it secretly and take it away
I would immediately tell him that
this pearl has no price

Han-Shan
translated by Arthur Tobias

TABLE OF CONTENTS

PREFACE

We live in a world of mystery, wonder, and beauty. But most of us seldom participate in this real world, being aware rather of a world that is mostly strife, suffering, or meaninglessness. This situation is basically due to our not realizing and living our full human potential. This potential can be actualized by the realization and development of the human essence. The human essence is the part of us that is innate and real, and which can participate in the real world.

This series of books, Diamond Heart, is a transcription of talks I have given to inner work groups in both California and Colorado, for several years, as part of the work of these groups. The purpose of the talks is to guide and orient individuals who are intensely engaged in doing the difficult work of essential realization.

The talks are organized in a manner that shows the various states and stages of realization in the order that occurs for the typical student, at least in our teaching method: the Diamond Approach. They begin with the states, knowledge, and questions most needed for starting the work on oneself, proceeding to stages of increasing depth and subtlety, and culminating in detailed understanding of the most mature states and conditions of realization.

Each talk elucidates a certain state of essence or Being. The relevant psychological issues and barriers are discussed precisely and specifically, using modern psychological understanding in relation to the state of Being, and in relation to one's mind, life and process of inner unfoldment.

Hence, this series is not only a detailed and specific guidance for the student, but also an expression and manifestation of the unfoldment of the human essence as it reveals the mystery, wonder, exquisiteness, and richness of the real world, our true inheritance. Each talk is actually the expression of a certain aspect or dimension of Being as it descends into the consciousness of the teacher in response to the present needs of the students. The teacher acts both as an embodiment of such reality and as a channel for the living knowledge that is part of this embodiment.

It is my wish that more of my fellow human beings participate in our real world, and taste the incredible beauty and integrity of being a human being, a full manifestation of the love of the Truth.

Richmond, California 1986

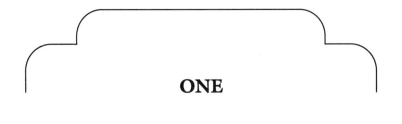

ONE

Hanging Loose

The process of freeing oneself can be seen from two complementary and interconnected points of view. The first looks at the process as self-realization, which is called self-actualization or essential development. The other point of view sees the process as liberation or freedom. Which perspective you emphasize depends on what you are aware of in yourself. There are two contenders for your attention: essence and personality, your true nature and your acquired identity. From the perspective of essence, self-realization means realizing or developing one's essence. From the perspective of liberation, the process is seen as becoming free from the personality. In our work, these two developments go on simultaneously; they are actually one process. In the past, different systems have emphasized one or the other to the extent that at first glance they may appear contradictory. Sometimes conflicts arise because of the terminology. Those who are on the path to self-realization say, "Just realize yourself, develop your inner potential. What is this enlightenment business? There's no such thing." Those who are seeking liberation or enlightenment say, "What is self-realization? There's no self to be realized. The concept of self is what you need to get rid of."

So far in our work we have not separated the two perspectives. However, we have approached the process of freeing oneself mainly from the perspective of essential development, of becoming more and more your essence. So now we will explore further the perspective of liberation and freedom.

This issue typically arises for people who have a taste of essence, some experience of their true nature, because the taste brings an appetite for complete liberation. Liberation or freedom is not really concerned with any particular essential aspect, quality, or state. It does not matter what essential state exists in the experience of liberation. If you are free from personality, you are free no matter what the state is. In the state of liberation the content of experience becomes unimportant. It is very ordinary. Nothing specific happens, no huge realization or mind-shattering experience. It is the most natural state. It is so ordinary and so natural that when we have it, we don't know we have it. It is so uneventful that almost everyone goes in and out of it frequently. There are no flashing lights or brilliant suns. There is no drama. Liberation is beyond the dichotomy of essence and personality, and because it is so uneventful, it usually escapes us. Its subtlety prevents us from recognizing it, or even from being aware that it is happening. It is not easy to talk about it because it is so ordinary; there is nothing in particular that is present or not present. It is a state you experience every day when you are not self-conscious or concerned with anything in particular.

When your mind is free, not concerned, or worried, or focused on anything in particular, and your heart is not grasping or clinging to anything, then you are free. The most characteristic quality is that there is no fixation on anything; you're not focused on any issue or experience. Whatever is there, is there. So there is a freedom of mind. The mind is not saying, "I want this," or "I want to look at this," or "It has to be this way." The mind is loose. The expression "hang loose" tells us what it means to be liberated.

Being liberated means there is no clinging to anything; there is no worry, no concern, no heaviness. The mind is not fixated, focused or bound to any particular content; you are aware of whatever arises in the mind, without effort, without even trying to be aware. You don't care whether you are sensing your essence, or even whether your essence is there. Whether you are happy or sad, whether a person is there with you or not, none of these things seem important. For the moment you're completely free from all the concerns in your life. This state can never be achieved by striving for it. It will just happen one day, and if you notice it you won't think it's a big deal. You'll go on eating your dinner or whatever you are doing. The moment it becomes a big deal, it's gone. The moment you have the attitude of, "Oh, wonderful! I want to know what's going on—I want to hang on to this," it's gone. Holding on is exactly what is absent in this state, and because of the tendency to grasp this subtle state, it can be very fleeting. It's very simple, the simplest thing there is. Young children are in this state much of the time, a state without concern for anything in particular, daydreaming or playing. But because of our early experiences, our minds become set in a certain direction, so that we fixate on a certain part of reality and reject the rest. This selectivity is the loss of the state. It occurs very early in life, but the fixation doesn't usually become dominant until age five to seven. Until then, the experience of this state comes and goes, but gradually is experienced less and less often. Throughout life it comes and goes, for some people more often than others. It is a state of release, but without a conscious feeling of release; everything is loose. This condition of freedom is not like liberation from some particular oppression; it is the raw state of liberation itself, so liberating that it doesn't matter what your experience is. You don't care what you're experiencing. Your heart is open and your mind doesn't fixate on preconceived ideas or worry about imagined possibilities. You're completely accepting without thinking or feeling that you're accepting. Essence will be there freely in whatever way your being needs at that moment, but still the presence of essence is not your focus, it's just who you are, what is present in your experience now.

We can talk about this state but we cannot say exactly what it is. You may realize that this is a very familiar state that you've been in many times. It's a very ordinary state; everyone needs to experience it in order to live and enjoy life.

What can we do to prepare ourselves for this experience, and particularly for the perception of the liberated condition? Everything we do here is of course contributing to it, but let's talk more specifically about the primary ingredients needed, what I'll call the factors of enlightenment. What are the primary factors that will prepare you for that perception—that subtle, fleeting perception? Ultimately, all the essential aspects and the knowledge and wisdom that comes from them are needed. Here we'll explore the seven primary ones.

First of all, you need energy, energy to work on yourself and work through the personality and its patterns. Energy is the sense that you have the capacity, the strength, the courage to do something about it, about yourself, about your life. You have the energy that makes you feel, "Yes, I can do something. I have strength, I have a spirit, I have potency." This energy will give you the fuel to look at yourself and understand things. Many things need to be understood and experienced; tremendous amounts of energy are needed, tremendous amounts of spirit, to be able to work through all the processes, and to deal with all the illusions that cloud the perception. So the factor of energy and strength must be freed and developed.

Another factor is determination. Without determination, the energy will be meaningless. You need steadfast determination and an unwavering will to go on, to continue in the face of discouragement and disappointment. Determination is what pushes you, what makes you persist. It is important to understand the personality issues around will and determination: what the issues are that make you feel castrated, that stop your determination, that block your will, that stop you from feeling, "Yes, I will do it." You need to discover what stops you from saying, "I'm going to do it. Whatever happens—disappointment, pain, fear—I'm going to continue. I might die before I do it, but I'm not going to stop. I'll continue after I die." With this capacity you know you can act in accordance with the importance of what you are doing.

Another factor that comes into the picture is a sense of lightness about the whole thing, a sense of joyousness. It is a specific kind of joyousness, a specific kind of lightness, a specific kind of delight. The delight and the joyfulness are the actual work itself. It is a delight in the truth, delight in seeing and experiencing the truth. It is a little like curiosity—a joyful curiosity about things. If you have only energy and determination, things can get a little heavy, ponderous, and very, very serious. The factor of joyousness is the lightness, the delight that opens things up. You become delighted to be doing whatever you are doing. This lightness has a curiosity to it, the way a child is curious. When a child is curious, he doesn't have a goal in mind. He's not thinking of getting a B.A. or a Ph.D. He's just curious at that moment. He isn't concerned about what will happen next.

The next factor needed to prepare ourselves for the perception of the experience of liberation is that of compassionate kindness. It is a very important, necessary quality. You need kindness for yourself because the process is difficult. Since you're not liberated, it is natural that you'll suffer, so why push yourself in a way that you'll suffer more? Why beat yourself up if you make a mistake? The factor of kindness also brings a quality of trust in yourself, trust in the process, a kind of trust in your mind, in your essence. Kindness also brings an unselfish attitude. If you have kindness, you have kindness for everybody, for everything. You have kindness for anything that suffers. You're doing the work out of kindness because you suffer. You see that you suffer, and out of kindness for yourself you want to do something about it, and that kindness in time extends to others. Other people's suffering hurts you too. You want to liberate yourself and you want other people to be free from their hurt and suffering. This natural course of events brings in a very important attitude that is a factor in allowing this state of liberation. This liberation has no fixation, and if you are focusing only on yourself, that is already a fixation, the biggest fixation. "What's in it for me, what hurts me, what doesn't hurt me, what's good for me?" Activity is focused around the I, the sense of ego identity.

Compassion is a vehicle that dissolves this fixation or boundary, and frees you from self-centeredness. Kindness makes the pain of going through difficult work tolerable, and brings more trust to your mind, your essence and your heart; it brings more gentleness into your work, and more compassion for others, and works on the dissolution of the self-centered fixation which is one of the main barriers to self-liberation. It is a very necessary factor which needs to be developed while we're working through the personality patterns and issues.

Another factor necessary in this work is peacefulness: the ability to be silent, the capacity to be still, not always in activity and noise. Stillness of the mind. In order to recognize true liberation you must have this capacity for stillness or peacefulness, because liberation is so fleeting. If you are thinking and worrying and planning and carrying on your normal fast-paced activities, you are precluding this experience from your life. As you develop and appreciate the stillness that leads to the absence of agitation, you allow a state of restfulness that leads to intuition, to insight, and to the subtle perceptions.

The next factor which is needed is the capacity to be absorbed in something, to be totally absorbed with whatever you're doing, in whatever state happens to be there. You become so one-pointed in your experience that you become completely involved in it, and so involved that you are dissolved in it. This is a certain kind of relationship to experience, a certain capacity, a certain freedom from the personality. The personality usually maintains a kind of separateness from experience. It is afraid of completely dissolving, of becoming one with experience. When you completely experience essence, there isn't an explicit experience; you are so absorbed in it that there is nothing but the essence. When you are working on making a table you are so absorbed in it that you, the tools, and the table are all one thing. There is no mind making a distinction or separation in the experience. You can be absorbed in an action, an emotion, a thought, a sensation, or an essential aspect. The Hindus call this state samadhi, complete absorption. In this state the personality is allowing itself to die, to dissolve, to become totally immersed, totally merged with whatever happens to be the experience.

The seventh and last factor of liberation is awakening, the capacity to be awake in your experience. We talked about the capacity to be absorbed in your experience; there is also the capacity to actually be awake, to be aware. You are so aware that you feel as if you have just awakened. There's a feeling of light all around you. The quality of awakeness is an antidote to sleepiness and to dullness of perception in doing the work. It is needed to understand the issues of your personality, and helps in dealing with attachments. You're awake to what's happening, not asleep to it; you're conscious. You are awake with clarity and light; things become clear and crisp. You see things as they are, what's there exactly, not what your unconscious sees. It's clear and light, like an open clear sky, the absence of fog. It's not as if the sky is clear and you are looking at it—you are the clarity. The mind is functioning with complete openness and clarity.

The combination of all these factors brings about objectivity. The seven factors—the energy, the determination, the joyfulness, the kindness, the absorption, the peacefulness, and the awakeness—come together in perfect proportion, and exist as one phenomenon, whose quality is objectivity. Objectivity is exactly what is needed to deal with the personality, its basic patterns and its basic tendencies toward grasping and attachment. With objectivity you are not influenced by your superego or your unconscious; what you see is what is there. You are not determined by your past experience, by concepts, or by opinions. Your strength is objective, your will is objective, your joy is objective, your kindness is objective, your peace is objective, your capacity to be absorbed, to be dissolved is objective. Objectivity takes the seven factors to another dimension, another level. The seven factors are called the lataif, the seven elements of subtle consciousness. The energy is the red latifa, the determination is the white latifa, the joy is the yellow latifa, the kindness or compassion is the green latifa, peacefulness is the black latifa, the absorption is the blue latifa, the awakeness that can free us from desires is what we call the clear latifa. The lataif are a very subtle kind of presence; some people say it's like air, a subtle air that produces those qualities in you.

The consciousness now is objective because it balances the seven factors, and is exactly what is needed to be free from the attachment and grasping that are the most basic characteristics of the personality. The objective consciousness, what we call the diamond consciousness, allows freedom from these aspects of the personality. The diamond consciousness is a panoramic consciousness, in contrast to the fixated focus of the personality.

If you could look at your difficulties and conflicts objectively, you would see they are nothing but resistance against that objectivity, against seeing things as they really are. You are attached to your attachments and you don't want to see things as they are.

You are attached more than anything else to your personality itself, to the way your personality functions, to your likes and dislikes, and patterns. You've lived with your personality for a long time and it's familiar to you. Even if you don't like parts of it, it's still familiar and dependable. So why leave it? You don't want to be free from it.

To be objective means you must see what role your personality plays. It is this objective consciousness that can perceive the state of liberation, because it doesn't have any of the clinging attitudes or obscurations that block the perception. These factors are called factors of enlightenment not only because they will lead you to objectivity and liberation, but also because they are present in the state of liberation itself. You are joyful, you are kind, you are energetic, you are determined, you're clear, you're awake, you're completely absorbed in your experience, you're peaceful. All these qualities are present together in the objective level, as the diamond consciousness, or the objective consciousness. When this diamond consciousness finally perceives the state of liberation, it just melts, becomes softer, delicate, liquid, relaxed, and flowing. There is no structure, no fixation, no holding this way or that way, no preference one way or another. It's not as if you're objective or not objective, or you're kind or not kind, it's none of those. They're all there in a sort of melted, free-flowing loose way. They're so loose, they're so free that you don't think of yourself as kind, you don't think of yourself as happy. The moment you say, "Oh, I'm happy now," it's gone. You are it and that's it. You're not concerned about it, you go about your business, have breakfast, read the paper, go to work, have a fight. It doesn't matter. There is total freedom. You have learned how to hang loose. You are liberated and you are awake. The quality of the clear light is important because you are awake and you know that you know. That's the moment of recognition. A child may be in a liberated state but doesn't recognize it, loses it and doesn't even know he lost it. But when you're an adult you recognize it, you're awake. That's why the Buddhists emphasize the clear light, the awakening, because it is an ingredient that is needed. You need the clear light to be awake in this state, and to recognize it. You're absorbed in it. You're not trying feverishly to hold onto it.

The seven factors ultimately make the eighth factor, which is all the seven in one, making an octagon. I talked about these qualities because they are the main aspects of essence constituting the lataif, and as you continue, you'll find that each of the lataif goes on to deeper levels. Each one is like a whole universe of its own. These are the seven primary factors needed for liberation, and are factors of the liberated state. They will help you finally to hang loose. So I think our talk today explains the relationship between the personality and essence, and how essence contributes to the freedom from the personality which in turn would be the liberation to enjoy essence. Any questions?

Student: Where does watchfulness fit into this picture?

A.H. Almaas: Watchfulness is a way to develop awakening. When you are awake you are watchful without being watchful. When you're a light bulb, you don't need to look. So awakening is called the perfection of non-watching. You watch and you watch and you watch until you become the watchfulness. Then you don't put any effort into watching, you're just awake. You don't have to look in order to see, just by being there you see. Then you don't watch any more. But first you need to watch for a long time. You have to develop watching until you become the watching.

S: Could you talk about the meaning of the word Ridhwan and what it has to do with liberation?

AH: Ridhwan is a kind of contentment which arises when you're liberated. Your personality becomes contented when you're free. Your personality itself is free from its suffering and conflict. Christ said you need to become like little children in order to enter the kingdom of heaven. Ridhwan, contentment, is the entrance into the kingdom of heaven. It is an aspect of essence.

Liberation is really nothing but the personality becoming free in the moment; the personality loosens its grip, lets itself just relax. When your personality hangs loose you become like a child and you enter paradise. In Arabic, Ridhwan is the name for the angel guardian of paradise. But it is also the condition, the actual essential aspect of contentment, satisfaction and fulfillment. Many systems don't discuss this, for good reason: talking about it to someone who hasn't experienced this liberation increases attachment and the attitude of grasping. In fact, describing how wonderful it is, describing heaven, can increase the misery and stuckness. This is why many systems just talk about learning how to hang loose. You might be in paradise, but if you don't know how to hang loose, you won't enjoy it.

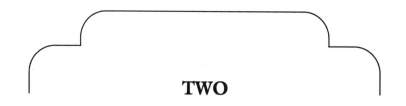

TWO

Mind and Essence

et us explore the word "mind." It is of course a common word, and we use it often in our work. In common use "mind" is an imprecise expression; not everyone uses it in the same way. There are cultural differences: in this country when we use the word "mind" it is not the same as what the Tibetans, for instance, mean when they say "mind." What we call "heart" in the west, people in the Far East call "mind." One thing we encounter is that the words "mind" and "heart" have a relationship which is not always clear. There are some people who use "mind" but mean "heart," and vice versa. When you read books or listen to lectures about "mind," you are always assuming a certain meaning, which may or may not be what the speaker or writer means; so it is natural that you will be confused. Let's investigate the meaning of "mind" beginning with the most generally accepted and most superficial meaning, and proceeding to the deeper aspects of what "mind" means.

The most common notion is that "mind" consists of your thoughts and thinking apparatus, and is connected with your brain. Generally speaking when people use the word "mind" in our culture they are referring to thoughts and images, things that pass through their heads, thought processes. So, usually it is understood to mean the thinking apparatus, or the processes of thinking, or the thoughts themselves.

But even in this culture, this meaning is not universal. For instance, in psychological literature this is not the meaning of the word "mind." Freud, for example, didn't refer to just your thoughts when he used the word "mind." Freud used "mind" to include all impressions, feelings, emotions, sensations, and not simply thoughts. All of these impressions are taken to be the content of the mind. In addition, of course, Freud postulated a level of mind he called "unconscious."

So the more technical use of "mind" in this culture is that the mind is the content of experience as a whole. All impressions are taken to be the mind. A further distinction can be made between that content and the container or apparatus that is concerned with these things. Either the content itself, or the receptacle or the perceiver of the content is considered the mind. This distinction is not generally made in psychological literature. If there is a distinction made, it is between the physical nervous system and the thoughts themselves. If you take the mind to mean only the mental processes, then the apparatus is the physical nervous system, the brain. If you take the mind to mean all impressions and experiences, then the apparatus becomes the whole body with the emphasis on the

entire nervous system including the spinal cord and gan-
glia as well as the brain. So now we have two concepts for
the word "mind." Of course, some philosophers talk
about the mind beyond the brain or nervous system.
They postulate the existence of a mind that operates
through the brain if they are referring to the "small
mind," or of a mind that operates through the whole nervous system, the entire "soma" or human body, which
they refer to as "big mind." The mind is seen not as
something definite, rather as a kind of force or agency. In
these formulations it is not very clear what that force is.

This leads to questions about the nature of the mind.
What is the mind that is separate from the brain and the
nervous system? Is there an agency of the processes? Is
there a force?

Within this culture and the West in general, outside of
academic or brain research domains, there is little exploration into this question. An exception is the religious or
philosophical idea of the Logos, which we will not discuss
here; the Logos is a metaphysical concept and here we
want to remain near to experience. In Eastern thought
"mind" means more than the mental, more than the
thoughts; "mind" means the whole apparatus, the whole
process, all the impressions. All the content of experience
is called mind. And, further, there is an attempt to understand what is the nature of the mind. Are these impressions self-existing, or do they occur to something, or in
something? Are these impressions part of a physiological
or electrochemical process that takes place in the nervous
system? Where do these thoughts, feelings, and sensations
come from? Especially in Buddhist thought we see a serious attempt to understand the nature of the mind, its
actual intrinsic nature.

In the West, psychologists have formulated models
of what they call the "mental structure" or "psychic

apparatus" to describe the structure of the mind. One such formulation is that there is a structure that develops from childhood to adulthood which becomes the structure of the mind. It is generally not discussed whether there is something separate, or apart, or beyond, or above that.

In many traditions of the East, we find that when they want to try to understand the mind, the "big mind," they don't look at structure. They try to understand whether there is a mind beyond the structure. Or is the structure the structure of something else? Does it exist somewhere, produced by something? This line of inquiry has developed many meditative systems which seek to understand the mind, to pay attention to all these processes, impressions. They want to know if that is all, or whether there is something else. What happens when the mind becomes quiet? When the activity is still, what will be left? It is reported that when you really go all the way through that investigation to its logical end, you find nothing. When all the thoughts, sensations, and feelings subside, and the whole content of experience is gone, you don't find the thinker, or the experience, or the container, or an apparatus. You don't find anything. This is labeled "the nature of the mind." In most Eastern thought there is general consensus that the nature of the mind is the void, a complete absence of anything. In this model, the thoughts don't come from anywhere and they don't go anywhere; they come from nothingness and go back to nothingness. The mind ultimately is a vast, boundless, limitless emptiness. There is such emptiness that it is not something which is there that is emptiness.

The nature of mind is seen as space, but even the notion of space must be transcended to deeply understand the nature of mind. As long as there is space, there is someone there experiencing something and calling it space. But completely experiencing the nature of the mind involves complete openness, or complete nothingness; when you really experience the nature of the mind, there is utter stillness with no observer observing anything, no experience, thought or label. Any experiencer would be just one of those contents, just a thought or feeling or constellation of thoughts or feelings. You continue finding nothing, you don't even find space; there will be space but no one to find it. This is sometimes called the ground of existence. In this perspective, then, the mind is taken to be everything, and the ground for everything. Everything is the mind because the mind is known in its most absolute nature as nothingness, as the absence of anything, which is seen as the ground for everything.

Nothing exists without that nothingness. Anything that exists needs some sort of space in which to exist. So, not only is it the ground of all experience, it is the ground of everything. It is seen as the basic nature of reality, as the deepest nature of reality. When everything quiets down, ultimately there is nothing. It is not that someone is looking, and can't find anything; in that process of looking, you start looking for yourself, and you don't find it. And finally, there is nothing. This doesn't mean that the physical body doesn't exist. There is simply no entity there producing, perceiving, or organizing these impressions, beyond the impressions themselves. There are simply the impressions that come and go; they come from nowhere and go nowhere. And then all impressions can cease, revealing complete emptiness. This is taken to be the most basic nature of reality, the ground of all existence. We call it space here because this experience is more like space. It is common to experience space with content as well, in which case space is not experienced completely. But if you allow yourself to penetrate to the source of everything, you will come to a nothingness or space. The nothing can go so far that there is also an absence of the consciousness of nothing. If there is consciousness of the nothing, there is still somebody there who can investigate, someone to ask, "What's that?" When you investigate further still, that also disappears, and then there is really nothing. So, nothingness as a space goes so deep that after a while it eliminates the consciousness of itself.

Because our normal consciousness can only experience things as someone experiencing something else, we cannot experience nothing without its being changed, mellowed down, bounded, because our usual awareness is very restricted and limited. Its tendency is restriction, limitation, specialization, labeling, and conceptualizing. The only way we can experience complete nothingness is for the usual consciousness to go. When it is gone, it is experienced as its absence, and its absence is seen as the absence of everything. It is not seen only as the absence of everything, but is also the absence of the absence of everything.

This experience is called cessation or extinction: complete death. It is what people usually think of as death. It is exactly how death is. You don't have to die physically to experience it. This does not mean necessarily that if you die physically you'll experience this kind of death. It is the complete cessation and absence of everything. As I said, this experience is needed partly because the personality has its own consciousness, which has to go. However, after it goes, it is possible for another kind of consciousness to be there to experience the complete, unbounded, limitless space as it is. There is a need for a complete, unbounded, limitless consciousness to experience nothingness. With your own consciousness, you cannot experience real unboundedness, real limitlessness. In the experience of the actual, unbounded, complete infinity of nothingness, your consciousness itself is unbounded, limitless, and infinite, which means not individual, not restricted, and not separate from what is experienced. When that kind of consciousness manifests, it is what is called cosmic consciousness, or universal consciousness, or primordial mind.

So we're seeing here another meaning of mind, which is pure consciousness. There is perception, but that perception is not of anything but the perceptivity itself. At this point we go into mind, not in the sense of it being just space, but of it being perception, consciousness. We see that we always have that consciousness. Every person, and every living thing, has this consciousness. In our everyday experience, there is always a consciousness of something; we never know consciousness by itself. There is always consciousness of the rug, my foot, my mind. Consciousness and the content of consciousness are never separate. Consciousness is always taken to be the content of consciousness, because that is how we operate with our limited consciousness. We never see consciousness in itself, in its purity.

To see consciousness in its purity is to experience what is called universal consciousness, to experience the mind as pure consciousness. When you experience the mind as consciousness, it is also knowingness, the very element of knowing. Either the individual consciousness has to go through the ego dying and then be reborn as universal consciousness as we described, or individual consciousness must expand to become universal consciousness. It's as if space experiences space, rather than someone experiencing space, and it is limitless. It is difficult to describe what universal consciousness or what the mind as consciousness means, because there are no thoughts in it. The moment there are thoughts, the content separates you from the consciousness. There are no thoughts; your head feels expanded, your consciousness spreads out

infinitely. It has no boundaries and no center. There is
not a somebody here looking at something there. The
looking is everywhere. Everything is consciousness existing as a universe of consciousness, boundless and infinite.

It is not possible to understand what universal consciousness is without experiencing it, because it eliminates
the ordinary level of understanding. The understanding of
universal consciousness is exactly the elimination of separateness, of any division in perception, including thoughts
about consciousness. There is no consciousness of anything
in particular. This is a foreign experience for most of us,
because we know consciousness only in terms of consciousness of something. In the pure experience of consciousness
there is no experience of body or thoughts; there is no
experience, no experiencer, no self. Hence springs the
Buddhist notion of no self. The Buddhists say that ultimately there is no self because in that aspect, universal consciousness, you cannot experience a self. Any entity-ness
stops you from experiencing this vastness which is the
elimination of separateness, the elimination of discrimination. There is complete non-differentiation. There is no
separation, no two, and no thought that there is one.

Ordinary, individual consciousness is actually based on
this non-differentiated consciousness. We use it continually, but we restrict it. This element of consciousness,
which is often experienced as a blue space or a blue light,
the most primordial element of knowingness, is also
called the origin of consciousness, the origin of knowledge; without it there is no consciousness or knowledge.
This is the closest that experience can come to seeing
knowingness as it is. This primordial consciousness is
taken by Hindus and some of the Buddhists to be the
nature of mind. This, then, is one concept of the nature
of mind: to think of it as consciousness, as a capacity or
the very nature or substance of knowing. Without it there

can be no knowing, no consciousness, no perception. In the process of becoming identified with our egos, however, we separate ourselves out from it, and then we never know it, we simply use it. When we relax the hold of the ego, our individuality, we can have a sense of non-differentiated consciousness in daily life. The discrimination and differentiation will return without the rigid separateness of the personality.

At this stage of unfoldment we encounter another aspect of essence, that is sometimes taken to be the nature of mind: clear discriminating consciousness, or seeing things as they are. We need this clear consciousness to function in the world. We cannot operate with only the level of cosmic consciousness; if there is nothing but "not two" you cannot even walk, or do any normal human functioning. But this perception can free your experience to incorporate the basic quality of non-separateness into your experience.

This development is called discriminating mirror-like consciousness. Everyone and everything is seen as it is. This is the realm of the mind in which it is seen that emptiness is form and form is emptiness. Your mind is spacious and empty; your consciousness is released so that everything is seen as it is. All the content of experience is seen exactly as it is, without a wish to manipulate, or label, or value things according to the unconscious. This is also experienced as clear mind, a sense of clarity and precision. Forms are exactly themselves, thoughts are just thoughts, feelings arise without impression or response, things are seen without the subjective filter. It is seeing things without the past, completely fresh and new. Cosmic consciousness is more primordial than this quality. Cosmic consciousness is the knowingness itself, the capacity to be conscious. In the mirror-like consciousness, the fundamental capacity for consciousness is functioning to simply reflect back what is there without distortions.

Primordial consciousness, the non-differentiated know-ingness, is the freedom that is needed for any state of the mind to be experienced in its most expanded form. It is the element of expansion into universality. For example, someone might experience a clear mind, but if they cannot experience non-differentiated consciousness then the mind is restricted to simply clarity in the head. If cosmic consciousness has been experienced then the mind is expanded, and the pure consciousness is integrated into the clear mind so that it is experienced as pure clarity, pure transparency, boundless and centerless. This boundless clear mind is sometimes seen as the emptiness itself or as the consciousness that perceives the void, since it is exactly what is needed to experience the void completely. So to understand the relation of the mind to the cosmos, we must first understand the nature of the mind, which we call space. Space cannot be known completely until the sense of separate mental consciousness is eliminated. When you as a separate person, as an individual, are completely absorbed into the universality of cosmic consciousness, then the mirror consciousness, the clarity, experiences the void completely and boundlessly. In the last chapter we referred to pure consciousness when we discussed the capacity for absorption, and to the mirror consciousness when we discussed the awakened state.

The void has been experienced and described in all these ways: as space, as blue consciousness, and as clear mind. As clear mind, it is then complete, transparent clarity that is aware of everything as it is, not as an undifferentiated medium that is cosmic consciousness, but as everything that exists as it is. It exists as that translucency. Everything comes back after it has been eliminated, and the emptiness is not touched, not eliminated by anything, even by thoughts, or feelings, or a sense of separate existences. Everything is part of that emptiness. Everything is seen as form, and any existence that is different from something else is just a form. The form is just one aspect of its nature, along with the transparency, the emptiness. This is the awakened mind; the Zen Buddhists call this awakening, space with no center, the nature of mind. Emptiness is not perceived by a separate individual; emptiness is perceived by universal clarity.

The awake, clear mind can go to sleep and still stay conscious. It has its night beside its day; its day is awakeness, its sleep is peace. It remains the nature of the mind, not as awakeness perceiving emptiness, but as peace, universal, unbounded, black peace, perceiving emptiness. Different systems emphasize one of three descriptions: the primordial non-differentiated consciousness; the awakened state of mind which is also universal; or the peaceful state of mind which is at rest, in complete peace. The nature of mind then can be experienced as blue, clear, or black aspects of consciousness. Each one of these can be considered a state of the nature of the mind. But we can say further that the nature of the mind is complete emptiness. We can experience complete emptiness as non-differentiated consciousness or as translucency, or as the night sky. There is always a subtle consciousness that perceives emptiness. The subtle consciousness can be restricted by your own personal consciousness, so that you don't see it as it is, or it can be expanded completely.

We have examined the understanding of "mind" from being seen as thoughts and thinking, to the bigger mind which is all impressions, to the nature of that mind as a whole as emptiness, and complete emptiness through the stages of universal consciousness, the awakened mind, and the peaceful mind. The non-differentiated mind is usually, but not exclusively, the emphasis of Hinduism. The awakened mind is usually, but not exclusively, the emphasis of Buddhism. The peaceful mind is usually, also not exclusively, the emphasis of Islam. Black peace is emphasized by the tradition of Islam. The center of the Kaaba to which prayers are directed is a black stone, a black block of peace. The word Islam comes from "salaam" which means peace. Mohammed's flag was black.

Understanding of the mind as emptiness and these basic kinds of consciousness, the primordial, the awakened, and the peaceful, are not metaphysical, or only of metaphysical interest. Without this understanding, there is no freedom for human beings, no freedom in any experience. It is due to the lack of this understanding that there is suffering. The mind must be understood completely if there is to be a release, or freedom, or peace. One is erased, then one wakes up, then there is peace.

As I said earlier, what is called "mind" in the East is related to what we call "heart" here. There is a relationship between mind and heart. The primordial consciousness, the awakened translucency, and the peaceful stillness of the mind are forms of consciousness which are also aspects of essence, and essence is the heart of the mind. When the word "heart" is used in the East, it means essence, the deepest nature of something, the heart of something, as in "the heart of the matter." The nature of the mind is emptiness, and the subtle consciousness that perceives that emptiness is the heart of the mind. But this relationship of the heart to the mind is even more complex. There is also the mind of the heart, the consciousness of the heart, the knowingness of the heart, the curiosity of the heart, and the sensitivity of the heart. The heart is seen as the sensitive organ, the knowing organ. It is conscious and perceptive. The heart is sometimes called the mind because the heart is the source of the heart of the mind. In this way, one could also say the mind is the mind of the heart. But their unity goes even further than the mind of the heart or the heart of the mind. They are the same. At the level of understanding the mind as a subtle consciousness, as an aspect of essence, there is no heart and no mind, there is only one thing. It is experienced as one consciousness with no separation of the centers. Seeing things as the clear mind comes from looking at things as mind, and seeing things as the clear nectar is taken from looking at things as heart; but it is the same substance. Taken as mind, we see it as awareness, as light, as consciousness. Taken as heart, we see it as love or joy. The awakened mind is clear joy when experienced in the physical heart. When freedom arises, the fulfillment is experienced in the heart. What is in the head or mind is the same thing that is in the heart, and feels like clear light or rich nectar and is the same consciousness.

What we call love is the same as consciousness, but it is experienced in the heart rather than in the mind, in the chest rather than in the head. It is also the same thing as will, which is experienced in the belly. Essential presence in the mind is often felt as a diamond, and in the heart is often experienced as a pearl. It is the same consciousness, seen from an objective, clear conscious level or from a personal heart level. If it is perceived at a universal, objective level it is seen as diamond consciousness. In the heart it becomes personal presence, the pearl beyond price, and rather than being seen as consciousness it will be seen as love.

Here then we see that there is a deeper connection between mind and heart beyond the personality; in fact they are one. You can experience clear nectar or a clear diamond, or blue nectar or a blue diamond, or golden nectar or a golden diamond, and so on. The diamond form is experienced as consciousness or clarity. The pearl in the heart is experienced as true personal conscious presence. You can experience both at the same time, since they are one; however, within different traditions different perspectives are emphasized. In the Far East the spiritual systems emphasize looking at things in terms of the perspective of the head, of consciousness, and the result is enlightenment. In the Middle Eastern theistic tradition the perspective of the heart is emphasized so it is viewed more as a love affair. It is the same thing.

So far we have explored many of the concepts of "mind." We've looked at the mind as thoughts and as impressions of experience; we've looked at the nature of the mind in terms of emptiness and the essential aspects that unfold from this space in the mind, the heart and the will. The natural movement of this understanding is toward unification.

We can see the unity of unities by understanding the secret of "Hu." Unity is called "Hu" in Arabic. So we understand the complete unity if we understand "Hu." As we follow the unfolding of our understanding and experience we have noticed a movement toward unification. Where is this coming from? Is there a force pushing us toward unification? Is there still a deeper nature of the mind we haven't yet fathomed? There is that which creates space. That is "Hu," that is the ground of the ground, the source of the ground. The biggest unity must be what includes the nothingness and the thingness, non-being and being, space and creation, non-existence and existence. That is "Hu."

Is there an agent of unity? Is there that which can only move toward unity, which is not only the nature of the mind and heart but the nature of everything? There is no mind or heart or will there, nothing but this. We've seen the movement of the mind, the consciousness of the mind and its connection with the heart, that they are one substance. We do see the mind as a kind of diamond clear expansive consciousness and the heart more like running rivers and nectars. There is differentiation, but we do see a movement toward unification. Our deepest, truest, most inner nature is that of unity, of complete unification with no discrimination or differentiation, and this deepest innermost nature must manifest as the transforming agent. This is what is called the elixir of the mind, or the elixir of enlightenment. It reveals itself in whatever form you need in order to learn about unity. If you are interested in the mind, it will reveal itself as mind. If you are more heart-oriented, it will reveal itself as heart. If you are action-oriented, it will reveal itself as will. It loves you so much it is willing to be less than itself so that you will learn about it.

So this agent of unification unifies through transforming your experience, your perception, your consciousness, your love. It is a continuing process of transformation and metamorphosis toward unification. We have talked about it so far in terms of inner experience. However, that experience towards unification will be reflected in your whole life: in your relationships, in your work, in your values, anything in your life. In time it unifies the inner and the outer, the action, thought, and feeling.

There is in you an agent of unification which is an elixir present in every human being, and without which there is no life. It is itself pure intelligence, and everything is a result of that intelligence. It includes even ignorance and suffering that results from ignorance. This primary first cause, this primary intelligence which every human being has, is itself the hope for unification, and the agent of unification. It is what goes through the process of unification, and leads towards the final result of the unification, the unity. It includes differentiation and the movement toward differentiation because even that is part of a bigger movement toward unification. Every living being has some intelligence, an intelligence that is pure brilliance. It is no longer a differentiated color; it is the brilliance of all colors. It is no longer a differentiated quality; it is the brilliance of all qualities. All qualities, all aspects, all things become radiant, luminous, brilliant —become their truest nature, brilliance itself. It is light upon light.

The innermost nature of everything which exists is this source and agent of unity. Without it, we wouldn't be human beings; we wouldn't be alive. It is the innermost nature of our being; and it is not something vague, but something actually substantial. You might not be aware of it, but without it you cannot read this or understand me right now. You can perceive it. It is amazing that the agent of unification is the same as the agent of transformation, that transformation is transformation towards unity. It is miraculous and mysterious. First it is revealed in experiences of the heart or mind revealing facets, qualities, or aspects. It allows you to see yourself as compassion, love, or clarity, but the way it shows you that is by it, itself, being that. "Hu" becomes, through the brilliance, that which is you. You are learning what is you at that moment. If what you need is enlightenment, it becomes clear light. It teaches first by unifying, by directing your experiences toward more unity. In time it will lead to the inner experience in which it manifests as the agent of transformation itself, the elixir. It is also called the philosopher's stone and the water of life.

The moment your personality allows it to function, it starts unfolding by transforming you from the inside out, including the impetus to work through your issues. It transforms you by showing you one facet after another. You need simply to allow yourself the experience, and see. It is the agent that moves transformation toward unification.

What do we mean by "it is finally the unification"? I mean that as it transforms in front of your eyes, it also transforms your personality more and more, so that you can accommodate it and allow it, transmuting from one essential quality to the next, the entire gamut of human unfoldment, until finally it manifests itself. It is all the qualities of fulfillment of mind, heart and will, and more. It is sometimes called the "Father," in the sense that it is the overseer, the umbrella, or source of all aspects, the all-protector, the all-knower. And it is no longer light or love or substance or space or existence—there is no analogy for it in physical reality. In physical reality we see differentiation only. We see qualities only in their differentiated form. We can see green representing compassion and aliveness. We can see red representing energy and strength. We can see clear space representing clarity. We can see yellow representing joy, and gold as truth. However, we can see further that each color, when it becomes very shiny, has luminosity; even black has luminosity. Space itself can have luminosity. Imagine that all these qualities shine even more, until there is only luminosity. The elixir of enlightenment is the luminosity itself. It is not the luminosity of something; the luminosity itself is the source of everything. Usually we think of luminosity or brilliance as a quality of something, as an intensity of a color or quality. You don't usually perceive it as self-existing. But in the essential realm, it is self-existing, and is the source of all qualities as the innate synthesis of them all.

So the unity of everything is complete radiance, complete expansion, completely itself. In its final free expression, it is pure blinding brilliance, so blinding that you are effaced. This brilliance can be experienced as a clarity and intelligence, as an exploding intelligence that shatters all darkness and ignorance. At the same time it is pure love, most delicate and soft, and in the same instant the strongest and most powerful will. It is not three different things put together, but all one, the brilliance of the aspects of essence, the source and inner nature of every living thing and of all creation.

From this perspective, there can only be unity. As you look at it from outside, before you attain the cosmic consciousness, you see it as brilliance in this or that. But when the separateness is effaced, then you are it, there is nothing else. Then all of existence is just that, and that is the brilliance of "Hu." When it is in the head you are drunk with sparkling brilliance. Completely drunk and completely awake. Your heart can only sing, can only be transported with the lightness of complete delight. The joy is in praising of Him. You realize, when the brilliance takes you to the unity which is the beginning of everything, that it was always there as you, your deepest nature from the beginning. Even if you look at yourself from the perspective of evolution, even as the amoeba, your innermost nature is "Hu." It has not only transformed you so that you know it, it has created you so that you know it. It has created you so that you sing its praise. It is beyond experience and non-experience. The question of observer and observed is completely erased. There is only dancing; the universe as a whole, including its deepest torture, is dancing. These thoughts can't reach it; it shatters thoughts. Personality is shattered. People glimpse it and faint, disappear. That innermost nature doesn't see itself as innermost nature. It is the "All" and the "Everything." It is the fact that is always there in us, that is the seed in us, moving us toward itself. The mind will not rest till it knows it; the heart yearns for it, and its movement is true will. There must be unity in you to move towards unity. There can be no experience of unity if it isn't already there. That is why the unifying agent is called the seed of enlightenment. Everyone has it. If you let it act, it will in time bring this complete unity.

The Sufis use the name "Hu" to refer not exactly to the brilliance, but to the Absolute, the ultimate ground and nature, the void before it is conceptualized as void or space. So we can more accurately say that the ultimate "Hu" is actually beyond color and consciousness. The Absolute is the unity before manifestation, while the brilliance is the manifest unity. We can say that the first manifestation of the Absolute is the brilliance, the inner intelligence. The ultimate is so mysterious that we can apprehend only a brilliance, a radiance as we approach it. This pure brilliance is the first intelligence, the unity from which differentiation arises. It is the beginning.

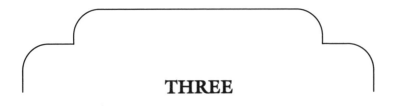

THREE

Implicit Understanding

When someone asked the Buddha what was the most important thing he'd learned from his enlightenment, he answered, "an implicit understanding." Today we'll try to understand what is meant by "implicit understanding."

When we are interested in inner development or self-realization, we are motivated to work on ourselves in order to remove the frustration and the suffering in our lives. We begin from a place of pain and we think the resolution will take place when we are no longer in pain. "I come here to work on myself because I feel miserable; when I start feeling happy, obviously, that means my problems are solved. So, teach me how to be happy all the time because that will take care of what I want."

Some people are straightforward with what's important to them, but most people disguise it. They'll say they want to know themselves better and experience essence, so they can use that understanding to find happiness. But what is this development and happiness they are after? What they really want is usually to improve in some way so their mother will love them, or their father will approve of them, or someone will think they're wonderful and fall in love with them. You can see that the basic motivation here is still to get rid of suffering, the suffering of not being loved, of not having approval, of being alone.

But the real cause of most of your suffering and pain and misery is ignorance. You don't know the nature of emotions and inner forces or how your mind operates; you act out of a lack of knowledge.

Now you say, "Good, let me have that knowledge and that understanding!" But you see the knowledge as a means to an end, and you believe the end is to feel good, to get what you want. This attitude, regardless of how much self-understanding you have, regardless of how committed you are to working on yourself, will only increase your suffering, because it is a result of ignorance about your true nature.

It is true that implicit understanding will release a person from suffering, but this is a side effect. It is not the main focus of our inquiry. As long as your perspective is to seek to feel good and not bad, to feel pleasure and not pain, you will reinforce your pain.

Now everyone is wondering, "Well, what are we going to do then?" But even this question is coming from the perspective of wanting to feel good. Who is asking the question? The one who is suffering and doesn't want to be miserable any more! So you're trapped. You can't do anything, you can't say anything, you can't think anything without reinforcing the basic perspective of wanting to be happy, wanting pleasure and not wanting pain. It's quite a dilemma: by desiring happiness you tend to create suffering.

Let us look further at "implicit understanding." The way out of our dilemma lies in the word "implicit." "Implicit" is not concerned with foreground, but underlies the foreground. "Implicit" is not what you are thinking about or trying to act upon, but refers to something in your very beingness. "Implicit" means the understanding is so much a part of you that it's in the marrow of your bones; it is part of the way you are, the way you feel, the way you think, the way you interact with people.

In the work here, you begin by understanding some basic things—your emotional make-up and your patterns and their connections. You start by observing and paying attention, and you find out certain things about yourself. As you know, this is not a mental understanding but an experiential understanding. Understanding your emotional make-up does not mean creating a mental description, but experiencing a deeply felt understanding. You experience what's there, and at the same time you see the connections between your emotions and your attitudes and your actions. This is necessary in the beginning. But by itself it is not enough. Merely understanding emotional make-up will not be enough from the perspective of implicit understanding.

Let's take the example of self-image. You discover you have difficulties and conflicts because you have a certain inner image or concept of yourself. You may see yourself as a weak person, or an ugly person. And if you believe you're a weak person, you will behave like a weak person. You won't do things you think only strong people do.

So when we identify a previously taken for granted self-image, we are able to see that it is just an image, it is not true. Some people believe that who they really are is a failure. They believe this so completely that they don't do anything successful people do. The moment they have some success, they become terrified. They feel it's not them; it's someone else taking over.

If you identify the self-image and understand it, you'll have some freedom from it. For example, suppose your self-image is that you're ugly. Your therapist says, "Look in the mirror." You look in the mirror, and you're not really sure. "Maybe it's not as bad as I thought. Maybe if my nose were a little bit shorter then I wouldn't be ugly."

But even if you can see the belief in the self-image, you won't be free of it, because on the emotional level you know this is a self-image only by comparing it with something else, another self-image. What is ugly? What is beautiful? You have your standard of beauty and according to that standard, you're not beautiful. Your superego tells you a beautiful woman is a woman with a small nose and that's it. If everyone tells you that your nose is fine maybe you won't think you're so ugly. But whenever you're feeling bad about yourself, you always remember that nose. If someone rejects you, you're sure it's because of your nose. The understanding that will release you from that self-image will come from a place that is not on the emotional level. A certain understanding is needed to eliminate the belief in self-image. This knowledge is that ultimately, you are not the self-image, you are not a concept; you are something else. And your nose, short or big, whatever it is, has nothing to do with who you are.

What I've just been talking about is written in all the books that deal with the matter of self-image. Buddha says, "You are not your self-image." "Oh wonderful," you think, "That's true, I'm not my self-image. So my big nose really has nothing much to do with who I am. Good. From now on I'll forget about my nose!" You forget for two hours. Then when somebody is looking at you the only thing you can think is, "Oh God, he thinks my nose is too big!" This person might be completely in love with you and think you're beautiful, but all you can think about is your nose. So it doesn't matter what you read, or what Buddha says or what anybody says, if you don't have the understanding that will eliminate the pre-occupation with self-image. The real understanding is something you cannot get from outside. Nobody can give it to you.

This is where essence is valuable; it will give you the knowledge and understanding that no one else can. If you deeply investigate the issue of self-image, you'll come to the essential aspect that corresponds to self-image. When this happens, you will experience essence in a way that has no self-image; instead there will be space, openness, inner spaciousness. This is the essential aspect that was lost when you developed a self-image and believed that the self-image was who you truly are. The self-image always has a boundary—physical, emotional or conceptual. When you experience space, you experience yourself as being without boundaries, without definition, just openness.

This essential aspect is itself the knowledge, is itself the understanding that your self-image is not really you. But until you experience yourself without self-image, there is no way for you to know that such a possibility exists, and you will continue to think of yourself in terms of your self-image.

We are seeing that the final knowledge needed to resolve this psychological issue is essence. It can't be resolved on the emotional level. On that level there is a piece of the puzzle missing, and that missing piece is essence. The essential aspect is what will provide the necessary knowledge for that issue and it will also be its resolution.

This is not news to most of you; it's what we call the Theory of Holes. I am explaining it again from the

perspective of self-image and space so that we will understand more. But this understanding is not implicit
understanding yet. In order to see what makes for
implicit understanding we need to talk about another
psychological issue, the issue of wanting love, or wanting
to be loved. As in the issue of self-image, you observe
yourself, your actions, your life, and you discover that
you have a need for love. You see your patterns, your
ways of trying to get love, the manipulations that your
personality has constructed to get that love one way or
another—by being a good girl, a strong boy, whatever.
Then underneath all this, you find that you want love
because your mother didn't love you. So far, so good; it
makes things clearer. You have some true understanding
of the situation. You know why you feel unloved, and
why you want love.

If you continue observing and exploring your feelings
around the issue of love, you'll discover a certain deficiency. You'll find that the need for love is an expression
of a part of you that feels deficient and empty. It is
always wanting to be filled from the outside. If you stay
with that wanting, allow yourself to feel the desire for
love deeply, you'll feel the deficiency, the hole of love,
and you'll experience the hole as the result of the loss of
your own love when you were a child. This will bring up
the hurt of not being loved, the deep wound; if you
allow yourself to experience this wound fully, it will
become like a fountain, a fountain from which love
flows. You will experience the aspect of essence that is
love. This was the missing piece that had to do with the
issue of love. Now you have love—not from the outside,
but from your own essence. Experiencing this essential
aspect of love erases the need to fill that emptiness from
the outside just as space or the void resolved the issue
around self-image.

However, this experience is not enough to resolve the issue completely. Many of you are aware of this. The desire for love, and the manipulations around it, may get subtler, but they don't disappear. This is because you do not have the implicit understanding. You have not approached your experience of love or space or any other essential aspect—will, compassion, pleasure—from the perspective of implicit understanding. You experience essential love, which is sweet, intense, and fulfilling, and you say, "This sweet feeling of love is the most wonderful thing I've ever felt. If it goes away, I won't have it. I want to hold on to it forever."

Who's talking here? What have you learned? You have had an experience of love, but that love has not transformed you. You have treated it exactly like any other object your personality wants. "If I have all this wonderful love, then people will see how radiant and loving I am and they'll think I'm wonderful and they'll fall in love with me and I'll live happily ever after." Nothing has changed. What you wanted from the outside, now you want from the inside, in order to get it from the outside!

This is not implicit understanding. This is materialism. Before, you wanted outer material; now you want inner material. It's all the same, all material. Before, you wanted to collect money, clothes, lovers; now you want to collect essential aspects: love, joy, will, strength. "Look at all these wonderful things I have! Now I can go and show them to my mommy and she'll finally see who I am and she'll have to really love me and then I'll be happy." It's the same thing. We didn't really go anywhere. That's where we started.

So what is the further understanding that is necessary? We have seen that the experience of essence provides an understanding that is not available on the emotional level.

When most people experience their essence, however, they treat it like something on the emotional level: a possession, a thing, a goodie. This is the basic make-up of the personality, to relate to things from the perspective of greed. It is this tendency of the personality to grasp for pleasure, even for the deep satisfactions of essence, which brought about all the losses in the first place. This tendency of the personality generates what it's good at generating—misery. Unless this tendency dissolves, your attitude toward essence will be the same as your attitude toward material goods. Your identity still resides in the personality, in greed, in suffering.

You're wondering what it is you have to do to gain the understanding and the freedom from the personality. "Oh, tell me, tell me what it is! Then I can do it—and be happy!" Do you see that tendency operating? The understanding is not there, let alone the implicit understanding.

You can develop a different attitude towards your experience. You can listen to it, and learn what it's like to come from a different perspective. You can experience the melting sweetness of love, for instance, and also listen to what else is happening along with that experience. "My girlfriend seems to be mad at me but I still feel I love her. That's strange. Usually when she's mad at me I can't stand it, but today she's mad at me and I'm not upset at all. In fact, I love her more. I can see and understand why she's angry. She's obviously hurt." You start thinking about a friend who was gossiping about you. You were mad at him. You wonder what happened to your anger. "When I think about him I just feel sweet. Isn't that something? Strange, I'm supposed to hate him but I just feel sweet. But wait a minute! It's not just him, it's everybody! I feel this love toward everybody! Usually I like somebody only if they're nice to me. But now it doesn't seem to matter if some people are nice to me or not. It's all the same thing. I feel the same toward all of them. That's pretty strange, isn't it?"

You might realize that your love has always been conditional. But love is not conditional. Love has nothing to do with the conditions of your personality. Love is who you are. Who cares whether somebody is nice to you or not? Are you going to stop loving because somebody happens not to be nice to you?

The next morning you wake up and you feel the love. Then you remember your friend who bad-mouthed you. "That bastard! Who the hell does he think he is, saying stuff like that about me!" Your girlfriend serves you breakfast and the eggs are over-easy, not sunny-side-up. "How come you can't remember that I like my eggs sunny-side-up? How come after all these months you still can't remember a simple thing like that? Obviously you don't really love me if you can't even remember how I like my eggs." And you stomp out of the house.

It's okay for this to happen. However, if you had learned from your experience of essence the day before, you would think, "Wait a minute, what happened? Yesterday all I felt was love toward my girlfriend and right now I want her to drop dead. That's interesting. I wonder what's going on?"

You have a choice: you can be open and interested about what's happening, and relate to it from the perspective of essence, or you can relate to it from the perspective of the personality, which means that you'll feel that you had something good and now you have lost it. You'll probably think you lost the lovingness because your eggs weren't done right.

If you related to this experience from the perspective of essence, you were looking, listening, questioning. You might understand what's making you feel the way you do, what's blocking your love, why it was there and then why it isn't there. You learn to allow your feelings to be there without necessarily believing them or acting on them, because you know there's just something going on you don't understand. You're aware that there's a lack of knowledge, there's ignorance. Otherwise you would not feel the way you do.

In time, this attitude of openness and allowing becomes a part of your daily life. You acquire an overall understanding of how feelings and events relate to each other, how things work, what makes you feel love at some times and not at other times. This understanding isn't just in your mind; it becomes part of how you act, part of how you are. You are not identified with your personality; you are open to understanding what your feelings are about, whether they bring you pleasure or pain. This is the implicit understanding: knowing, and acting on the knowledge that essence has a wisdom which can be imparted to the personality and thus transform it, releasing the barriers against the deeper understanding. Essence teaches you in a fundamental way; it provides wisdom that cannot be provided by anything else. If you are totally present for the essential aspect of love, it will be obvious that love is anchored in you, that it has no prejudices, no preference, no selfishness.

Gradually, you come to understand that the personality itself, with its characteristics, its tendencies, and its preferences, is the problem. If you relate to essence from the perspective of the personality, of wanting only what makes you feel good and not questioning it, of not wanting what makes you feel bad and not questioning that either, you feed the tendency of the personality for greed; you make your personality more opaque. Lacking some essential quality, not having something like love or value or joy, is not the problem. The continual presence of the personality with its patterns is the problem. And that can change only if you learn from essence, if you allow your personality to be transparent to essence, regardless of what feeling is there.

From this perspective of implicit understanding you see the work going through several stages. First there is the personality without an understanding of essence; then as you see the patterns of the personality you can disengage from those patterns and realize essence. This second step allows essence to act on the personality to transform it. Then there is the final transformation of the personality—the implicit understanding. Even when there is no particular essence manifesting, the personality is exactly like essence, completely empty of its patterns. It is then a transformed soul.

First you realize your essence and then you let go of your attachment to essence. This is the only way the personality can learn. Eventually, there is only implicit understanding, the understanding of how things really are. At first you think love means such and such. But when love is completely embodied and integrated, being a loving fullness or being a nothing becomes the same thing. The attitude toward feeling loving or feeling empty is the same.

It is true that we need to realize essence, to free and establish all its aspects. But this is not to make the personality better. It is not so that the personality can say, "Oh great, now I'm enlightened. Now I have this and this and this which I can use to get what I want!" No, the point is that the personality itself finally realizes its own bankruptcy and that its very existence is the problem. This realization cannot occur without the presence of essence; this is the value of essence. You can go to one teacher after another, you can read hundreds of books and have all kinds of insights, but this won't transform you until the knowledge itself, the understanding itself, becomes essence. Your personality can learn only when essence is actually there. You cannot know what love is unless love is there. You can't know what compassion is unless compassion is there. The quality itself, the aspect itself, and its wisdom and understanding need to become a part of your fabric. Then you'll be compassionate without feeling compassionate, you'll be loving without feeling loving, you'll be precious without feeling precious, you'll be all the essential qualities without feeling that any of them are there. The personality itself will become the implicit understanding. There will be no issue around wanting one thing and not another. What you do, how you live your life, is then simply according to reality.

What I have been talking about is a perspective on the kind of relationship we can have to our work, to our essence. Essence does not disappear; it will remain with you, as you, but without concern about it. Where there is concern, it is the personality which is concerned, even if the concern is about essence. When you first start working on your personality, you have to be concerned about essence; you need to understand your concern until you're no longer concerned. Then you can hang loose.

I can put this in a few words. Personality without essence is suffering. Personality with attachment to essence is a disaster.

Personality can become simply a transparent vehicle for essence. This transformation occurs through the knowledge of one's true nature—essence, the preciousness of Being—becoming so integrated and metabolized that it is second nature. This, then, is implicit understanding.

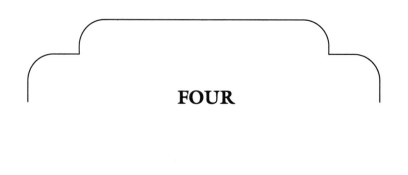

FOUR

Attachment and Space

I f you look at your life, what do you see filling it? Whatever you look at, whatever you think, whatever you pay attention to in your life, it is there, and you would like to have more of it. It is something that is easy to get, so easy that you keep accumulating it endlessly. You can't imagine living without it. Life without it seems like nothing; there is no point, no value in anything without it.

Everyone's favorite thing is attachment. If you look at yourself, your personality, mind, feelings, relationships, you'll find that attachment is omnipresent in all these aspects of your life. You try to fill your life with this or that all the time, whatever it is that you like. Of course, you don't think consciously that this is what you do. You don't usually think that what you are accumulating is attachment.

You think that you're filling your life with things, or the objects of attachments, but all of these things are always there in the world. What you fill yourself with is the attachment to them. The things that you are attached to change; you're attached to one person, another person, a third person, one car, another car. Whatever it is, physical, mental, or spiritual things, you shift the objects but the attachment stays the same. You always want to fill yourself with attachment; you can't imagine living without it.

If you look at yourself at any moment you will see your attachment. You might be attached to your present feeling, or to a thought, a dream, an experience, or to a certain kind of consciousness, but it is all attachment. The attachment is really much bigger than any of the objects of the attachment. It is omnipresent, and omnipotent in your life. It is what runs you. To accumulate attachments is very easy, and you continue to accumulate them all your life.

Of course, you don't experience attachment itself, because you are focused on the object of attachment. You're thinking of the person, or the feeling, or the object, or the experience you're attached to. You think that the object is what you want, but what you actually get is the attachment to it. If you could experience directly what attachment is, and feel just how it feels, then you would stop being so enamored of it. You would understand why your life is full of pain and suffering.

What do you think you're going to get from attachment? First we'll look at what you believe attachment is, then we'll look at what attachment actually is, and the levels of attachment and how to be free from them. Suppose you are attached to another person; this is a typical object of attachment. Let's be even more concrete: you're attached to another person's body. Attachment to that person or that body is not the same thing as liking the person, or enjoying the body or person; not the same as loving the person. We sometimes say we are attached because we love someone. But the attachment is a posture or an attitude of holding on to a person, an inner posture of grabbing, not wanting to let go.

Attachment is the opposite of separateness; it is wanting not to separate, wanting to cling, to possess. When you're attached to something or somebody, you behave like glue, you are sticky. You don't want to lose your object of attachment. What you want is a kind of connection, merging, or union with the object of your attachment. If you are attached to someone's body, you want union with that body. When you're so attached to someone, you start feeling "I just want to be completely one with you, no difference, nothing to separate us forever and ever—one body." In songs, stories, and novels this love is idealized: to find your other half, to be complete, to be one. To be so attached, so connected, so much merged, that there is no other and there is no you, no subject and object. You want that to go on forever. Whoever is the object of your attachment, whether you love the person, or like him or her, or are afraid of or hate the person, you always hold on. This is an example of love attachment.

You can be attached to anything that you think gives you pleasure or security: a dream, an idea, a thought, a feeling, a person, a car, a house, etc. Some are even attached to hate. A deep root of attachment is the desire for complete unity. On the surface you might just feel that you want something in a casual way, but if you look inside you, at the movement of attachment itself, you'll see that you really want to be one with it, and you try to get that by grabbing. Sometimes it's called the octopus state, and that's exactly what attachment is—"I love you, you're so yummy"—wanting to consume someone. It looks like a sticky mechanism which is holding on, or eating the object. A love attachment is often motivated by a desire for merging or union or connection, and you might even believe that you're getting them. But what you get instead is attachment, because real merging, union or connection doesn't happen with that attitude of grasping.

Attachment involves one thing attaching to another, a subject attaching to an object. The desire is for loss of the boundaries, but in attachment boundaries are created, because you make two, one attached to another. "I" want to have "this." So there is an "I," there is "this," and the "I" wants "this" forever. This is a misunderstanding of what union or connection is. Real merging means the boundaries between the two are gone completely. Then there is no one attached to another, no one holding onto someone else, no octopus with its prey; there is only one thing.

Ultimately, attachment is caused by desire and fear, desire for the good and fear of the bad, desire for pleasure and fear of pain, desire for life and fear of death. If you examine fear and desire you will see that fear itself is based on desire, fear of death is desire for life, and that its opposite, fear of life, is desire for death. Desire is there because of the absence of understanding. What will free us from attachment is understanding, or knowledge of how things really are. So we could say that attachment is based on fear and desire, fear is based on desire, and desire is based on lack of understanding or ignorance. If we are ignorant, we end up being attached. We are ignorant of the actual fact that union is the absence of boundaries. We create more boundaries with our attachments, which then stop us from getting exactly what it is we think we want.

From the outside, attachment is seen as an attitude of grabbing, of holding on to the object of desire; it necessitates the presence of both subject and object. By its very nature attachment is based on the belief that there are two, while what you want is one. Of course, it is not easy to understand exactly the relationship between this oneness and this duality, because oneness is not your usual object of desire. These objects of desire are just reflections of reflections of reflections of the original oneness or wholeness. When you go through the levels and see what the object of your desire is, your final object of desire, then you'll understand completely this dichotomy between "the one" and "the two." But now, if you want a car, it's hard to imagine that you want to be one with a car. At the deepest level, that is what you really want if you are attached to a car. So what do you want from the car? You want a good feeling, right? You want somebody to think you're wonderful, that you're rich and you think well of yourself. Why do you want that? You want pleasure and approval. And why do you want that? So that you'll feel harmony; for approval will bring a feeling of harmony which is a certain kind of free existence without limitations.

All attachments are in the end attachments to one thing. All our objects of desire are ultimately transferences, displacements from the original object of desire. Attachment is a misguided attempt to get to this oneness. You think you want something and you attach yourself to it. So you accumulate things—your clothes, physical appearance, boyfriends or girlfriends, husbands, wives, children, parents, art, creations, feelings, experiences, essence, personality, etc., anything that can be objectified becomes an object of desire. Attachments necessitate objectification; there has to be an object to be attached to, and by its very definition there is a loss of the oneness. When we see this we can see that even God becomes objectified and an object of attachment. If you look at your usual experience, everything in it is an object, and you are attached whether you like it or not. If you like something, it's a positive attachment, you're holding on to it. If you don't like something, it's a negative attachment, you're pushing it away. There is attachment in the rejection; by trying to push something away you're trying to hold on to something else in yourself. This is the external manifestation of attachment, what it looks like from the outside. But these feelings of wanting are not what the actual attachment feels like. You might feel that you can't let go of someone or something, that you love it, that you would feel a great loss if it were gone. Most people can only focus on the object of attachment; if they really saw the attachment itself they would start falling out of love.

So we can ask now, what is attachment itself? First of all, you'll need to see that all of your suffering, especially emotional suffering, is because of these attachments. If you're attached to anything there is suffering for fear of loss of it. If you have something, you're afraid of losing it; if you don't have it you are frustrated and suffering the absence. There is no rest or peace because something always has to be done to keep the desired object there. This frustration, this attachment is the essence of suffering. Directly feeling this attachment itself reveals it for the suffering and hell it is. It even feels like fire and brimstone—hot and irritating, caustic. It is the source of suffering because it is pure frustration, pure pain, pure dissatisfaction, pure nongratification, pure anguish. We have called this state negative merging because though what you want is true merging, what you get is negative merging.

Negative merging is not really merging; rather, it is two trying to be one while still maintaining twoness. Since this can never happen, there is always frustration. When I say that the negative merging, or the attachment, is hell, it doesn't mean that freedom from it is heaven. We think of heaven as pure nonsuffering, peace, rest, comfort, gratification, fulfillment. All of these things are what we call essence. However, if you are attached to essence, what do you increase? Not heaven—you accumulate hell. We cannot try to free ourselves from hell in order to go to heaven. What we need is to objectively understand the root of this vicious cycle of attachment. We need to see the basis of all this suffering for what it is. When attachment itself is experienced without the object of attachment, without attention to what you want to have and want to hold on to, when the sensation itself is felt, it is experienced as deep anguish, totally intolerable. We normally avoid this experience by not focusing on it; whenever you are attached you are in this suffering but you don't know it. So the obvious question arises: what can we do about it? But where is this question coming from? From our attachment to pleasure, our wanting to avoid pain and frustration. But this is the very nature of attachment, the very source of all desires, the Ouroboros eating its tail.

It is not easy to grasp this whole picture. And it is not easy to be free from this cycle. You must completely understand your situation, everything must be understood and felt, so that you finally see what the whole picture is all about. Then you finally understand what attachment is. But even now that you have heard this, you will continue living your life being in love with attachment, because so much of your attachment is unconscious. This discussion is only an orientation.

The very holding onto heaven is the hell. Pain is not separate from pleasure, heaven is not separate from hell. Psychological pain is just the attempt to hold on to the pleasure itself; this is the origin of all emotional pain. Of course the mind doesn't think this way. The mind thinks that if there is something you like you go after it, and that's the way to get it. If you have something you like, you hold on to it and that's the way you keep it, otherwise it will go away. The mind doesn't know true reality, it is based on ignorance.

How does attachment manifest throughout our lives? It manifests in all areas, in all corners, at all levels, in all its gradations. One of our deepest attachments is to our self-image, both how we see ourselves and how others see us. Our self-image is who we think we are, how we want to be, what we want to have in our life—whether it's a house that looks a certain way, a certain lover or mate who fills certain criteria. "I'm a good person and deserve this," or "I'm a bad person." The self-image we are attached to is often negative. Everyone has some negative self-image. If you're attached to being good, then you're always finding proof that you're a good person. You might be attached to a self-image of being good, strong, powerful, rich, beautiful, popular, being married, single, etc. This is the most superficial layer; and it's where most people live. The most common level of consciousness is focused on this superficial image level.

We usually identify with our self-image; we think that's who we are. This question of identity with what we think we are is at the root of attachment. What we ultimately want is to fight for who we really are, to actualize, protect and defend who we really are. We want to make what we really are permanent and, depending on our knowledge of what we actually think we are, that's what we get attached to. In the beginning, identity manifests as the self-image, and most of humanity seems to be concerned with this level. Your identity is very much invested in the image, how things look on the outside, and that's what you're attached to. The self-image gets fed by myriad attachments, from your earrings to your friends, from your interests, likes and dislikes to your ideas and feelings, your philosophies, all of your conscious awareness at any particular time. The work we do here, on the other hand, is on the dissolution of the self-image. What we mean here by dissolution is simply seeing that it isn't actually there. The dissolution of a certain identity is finally seeing that it is not really who you are, that the life that you have created around you is not really you. You believe that you can't exist without it; that without these ideas, these things, these attachments, you would not be you. "How would I know myself?" you wonder, "How would anyone know me?"

So the first level of attachment goes along with the first level of identity. It has to do with your I.D. cards. It is very clear that the image gets bigger the more cards you have. If a person wants to change his image he gets a different kind of card. In modern times people really think like this; when you get out your wallet your importance is measured by how many, or what kind of cards you have. If you don't have cards you can't get in. If you go to any federal agency and don't have a birth certificate, they will ask you to prove you were born. In a bank, all the cards prove you amount to something. This influences our minds; indeed, it influences the mind of the whole culture. Only when we see that there is a part of our minds that does believe this is there a chance to dissolve it. Just seeing that, "Oh, I believe that is me," and checking, "Is that really me?" will make the identity more transparent. The sincerity and the understanding dissolve the self-image, just as any untruth dissolves when the truth is seen. When any self-image changes there is a sense of freedom, the emergence of what we call space.

When there is space, there are no pictures, no boundaries. An image requires boundaries; it's a picture of who you are. So space erases your boundaries; it erases the picture on your driver's license, so to speak. You come to know yourself without the card. When you have no picture of yourself, there is space, the first level of the void.

At the next level of attachment, the core of the self-image is the body image. At the deepest level, your self-image is based on physical reality, the body image. When I say "body image," I include in that the shape of your body, how you feel about it, everything about your body, the organs of your body and the functions of your body. When you let go of the external card-holder identity, you find that then your identity is based on your body image, so you sense yourself, feel yourself, pay attention to yourself and feel that you know yourself more intimately. If you think you're beautiful, you like yourself; if you think you're not beautiful, you don't like yourself. You're fat or you're thin, you've got the right nose but the wrong mouth, or vice versa. The intimate things become very important, whether you've got a penis or a vagina. "How big is my penis?" "Are my breasts big enough?" "Oh, I want a girlfriend with big breasts." "I'm going to work to get my body in shape." These are the obvious body image concerns; it is part of the self-image, a kernel around which the rest of the self-image is built. It is attachment to physical things from the image perspective. The image of physical objects is present, not only image in the sense of shape, but also in terms of feeling, function, and relationship to your body.

If you go to the level of dealing with the physical or the body image, you will see that your body image is not accurate. Most people don't see their bodies, even in terms of shape, the way they really are. Many beautiful women don't see themselves as beautiful. From these distortions in our self-image we build all kinds of psychological self-image compensations: I want to be beautiful, dress this way, cut my hair like this, have certain kinds of friends, have this kind of environment around me, get the best fashions, the whole thing. But at the bottom of it is a certain misperception of the body image. We need to understand the body image, to actually see what is really there, because the identity is very much involved with it. Understanding the body image, seeing your unconscious body image, contrasting it with what is actually there, corrects the misunderstanding. It will also eliminate the attachments, because the attachments arise from this mis-understanding. And this will bring in the next level of the void, what we call the dense space, because the body is dense compared to the self, and it is felt or sensed in this way. So another level of space will come that will erase or correct the body image by understanding the body image, which will itself eliminate the attachments to the body image, attachments on the level of the physical image. Now the truth emerges that I am not my physical image. First we free our identity, our external self-image, then we free ourselves from the external body image. It's not a matter of whether I'm ugly or beautiful, tall or short, graceful or gawky. It's not that I have a big penis and that's why everybody likes me, or a small penis and that's why nobody loves me, it's not that you have or haven't got something. The way my body appears does not define who I am.

The next layer of identity is what we call the internal body image, or identification with the body regardless of the image, attachment to the body itself. Internal body image forms the core of the identity at this level, because of identification with the actual sensation of the body, the actual feelings in the body. It forms the core of both the body image and the self-image, and you're in touch with it most of your life. The inner sensations of the body —how it feels, the warmth or cold, harshness or softness, pleasure or pain, the flow and rigidity, the tension and relaxation—all become part of the identity.

This identity with the internal body image creates attachment to the body itself, to physical existence itself.

You need to understand that this is not your identity. You are moving beyond an image here, these are your physical "innards." This identity is more intimate. You need to correct the common misunderstanding that to be your body, or to have your body, you have to hold on to it. You find out at some point when you're studying your attachment to your body, that you believe you have to hold on to your body to have it. You believe you need tensions in order to feel your body. If you were to completely relax, you would feel you were going to lose it, float away, so you grab on! That grabbing is the tension, and going deep inside that tension you will feel the actual stuff of attachment, which is hell.

So you need to come to an understanding of your relationship to your body, how you identify with your body and your attachment to your body as a result of that identification. You think your body is you, and you hold on to it for dear life, so you're never relaxed. This level includes all the attachments to all the bodily pleasures, and the negative attachments to all the physical pains. It includes sexual pleasure, physical contact pleasure, movement pleasure, stillness pleasure, all the realms of bodily attachment to pleasure and lack of it. Attachment to the body then is not just attachment to the physical body, but also to what the physical body means to you, all the pleasures and the comforts and the safety you believe it gives you. There is nothing wrong with these things, it's the attachment to them that creates the misunderstanding that is experienced as frustration and hell. I'm not saying you shouldn't want all these pleasures, that's not the point. The point is, the attachments to them will inevitably cause suffering.

Becoming free from this attachment has to do with becoming free from the attachment to pleasure, all kinds of pleasure. It is the loss of attachment to physicality, to your body from the inside. It's not a matter of image here, but of direct sensation, direct feeling. This identification is very intimate; it is something you've lived with all your life, and you always believe it's you. Ultimately, it gives you comfort. When you see this identification for what it is, it also will dissolve, because it isn't any more real than your driver's license identity. This realization in turn brings in a new space, a new awareness of the void, what we call "death space." At this point a person experiences what is called death. It is what happens when somebody dies physically; they actually disconnect from the body. Death is a deep dark black emptiness; of course, this death space can be experienced in life. You don't have to physically die; all that is required is to lose the physical attachment to the body, and the death space will be there. You will know what death is, you will know that you are not the body, and then the identification with the body will be lost. You will know what it's like not to be connected with the body. At a certain level of realization, if you are conscious when you're physically dying, then you will see that you're not your body because you're still there. There is consciousness, but the body is gone. Then you know that death is just a transition. It can happen in normal life without physical death. It simply means the loss of the physical attachment to the identity with the body. When you know that your identity is not the body then a new level of the void emerges, the black emptiness. Each level of dissolution brings in different experiences of the void, different grades of space.

When the attachment to the body is understood, all the attachments begin to dissolve; you know that it is not you. You know you would exist without it. The need for the attachment is gone. Then there is no fear and desire that will lead to the attachment to that particular body, to that particular level of identification. When the attachment to the body is understood, and you go through the death experience, you know you are not any of these things, images or sensations, and you see the true identity of essence, the true self. This is death and rebirth. This is referred to in the The Tibetan Book of the Dead: if someone is conscious during the death experience then self-realization will occur. You are aware of your true identity.

The true identity will expose the false identity, the personality. So the death experience is needed to see the true identity, which in turn will reveal the false identity, what most people call "myself." There are many other levels. When you ask people "What is your self?" they respond according to their level. At the surface level someone will call their card-holder identity "myself." If someone is at the body-image level they will call that image "myself." If you are sensing your body at a deeper level you will call those sensations "myself." There are many other levels. If you pursue this question of who you are, what is your self, you may discover that none of that is really you. But to know that, the true identity must be there, to make the contrast. Then we can directly experience the very subtle psychological identity, which we call "the pea." Everyone has a pea. The pea is what is called ego identity in psychological literature, and in spiritual literature it is called "the ego."

So the death experience we have just described, the dissolution of the identity with the body, does not necessarily mean the death of the ego. The death of the ego itself is a deeper thing. You may know that you aren't your body, but you still have a mind, an ego. You are now attached to your inner experience, experienced as somewhat disembodied. You're attached to your psychological identity, your psychological makeup, to all your thoughts and feelings. This is the source of all the other identities. The self-image, the body image, the body identification all emanate from this kernel, this pea of identity. This finally is the ego. This is why people who die are not necessarily free from the personality, the ego identity, because even when they die consciously they are not free from the mental configuration, mental existence, their personality. This means that a person can experience ego without a body before he dies. The moment you see that you're not your body, it is possible then to see the ego, finally to identify the center of the personality—the ego that we call "myself" or "I." When you say, "I'm doing this," "I want this," you are attached to this sense of self. That is the deepest attachment. These attachments are there all the time; we see each one under the last one but they all exist simultaneously. The deeper attachments are the strongest. We aren't usually aware of them, because we can see only what we allow to be conscious. Of course, the ego identity, the "I," is still not truly who you are. You can identify a certain interaction between the true self and the false self, and this will help you to see what is really you and what is not you, what is your personality.

In our work, we use the true self to expose the false self. But there is always the danger of trying to hold on to an identity. The Buddhists, for instance, don't talk about a true self, because they see this danger. They say there is no such thing as a true self, because your belief in a true self might enhance or substantiate an experience of ego. Here, then, we see the need for the dissolution of identity itself, whether true or false. We are attached to identity itself, and any attachment to identity, even to an experience of true self, becomes the false identity. We want to hold on to identity because we assume that we need a center. "Now I have a true center," says ego, "finally I'm self-realized." The ego is gloating over its victory, "I have slain the ego," says ego. "Now I am a star, I'm no longer a human being," says ego.

Then the next level of the void needs to arise, the level of the dissolution of identity. We need to see that the attachment to identity itself is also hell and frustration. At this point you begin to see hell more clearly, more palpably. You start burning. The more attached you are to that identity, the more the burning and frustration. Then the dissolution of self, or the dissolution of identity, is what we call extinction, annihilation or nonexistence, which is a new level of the void. Not only your body is gone, but also your identity, your ego is gone.

The only possible way to regain Oneness, the original oneness that we want, is to allow the identity to dissolve. The separate identity needs to go, even the true identity. Attachment to the true identity will keep you separate because attachment creates boundaries. The boundaries need to be lost, and the boundaries can only be lost by the loss of identity itself, by the loss of the separate self. When that goes, then it is possible to see that you are not separate from the original consciousness, that there is only one consciousness, one existence. That is what we call the cosmic level. At this cosmic level you understand that true merging is a loss of your boundaries, so you are One. If there's a sense of identity, there is not One. You might perceive the cosmic consciousness, but if you are not dissolved in it you can still be attached to it. When there is no individual identity, no boundaries, you will know that what you have always wanted is this dissolution, merging into One. To merge means to lose your self, without holding onto something; you have to lose yourself completely, even your desire, your wanting.

After ego extinction there is cosmic identity or cosmic consciousness. Now the identity, the ego is gone, but there might still be attachment. We have dissolved the roots of attachment, fear, and desire but the process of attachment itself, the actual activity of attachment can exist without a center. One can have a very subtle attachment to the cosmic identity. It doesn't even feel like attachment. You can experience God, which is what's called the cosmic identity, but as long as you want only that there is still some preference, some attachment. Now the identity is seen as the cosmic ocean, but there remains some identity, though it's not personal. On the personality or essential levels there is no identity, but the cosmic identity is still there.

Now there is need of another level of the void to eliminate the final attachment, and we need to do nothing but see and understand this attachment to the wonderful cosmic existence, the all powerful, our truest nature. It is your truest nature, but the issue of attachment is not whether the object you want is good or bad, but that the movement of attachment itself creates separation and suffering. As on all the levels we have described, nothing needs to be done or can be done except to understand. True understanding will spontaneously bring in the deeper level of the void, which is complete, utter emptiness. There is no question of attachment to anything because there is literally nothing to be attached to, there is nothing. There is no image, no body image, no body, no personality, no essence, no God, no existence, no nothing.

It's hard to visualize what this means; in fact, many of the things I say are hard to imagine. The issue here is not what you are attached to. What is needed now is to understand the attitude of attachment itself, regardless of object, even if there is nothing to attach to. Attachment can exist at the level of the cosmic existence as a remnant of personality, although the identity with the personality is gone.

In this case you could say that the ego has gone but the personality remains. The personality has in a sense become the cosmic personality, infinite, boundless. This final identity is the cosmic identity.

If you can disidentify from your cosmic identity, then what's identifying, what's disidentifying? As long as you can disidentify from any experience it is not the final freedom. If you can disidentify from something then you can be attached to it. It means there is some object or way of objectifying an experience to identify with or disidentify from. As long as there is any sense of identity there is a possibility of attachment, because there is a possibility of wanting to hold on to it. At this level, the question of the cosmic identity versus the big void delineates the difference between the world's theistic and non-theistic religions. The theistic religions believe in God. The non-theistic religions adhere to the emptiness, the cosmic nothingness. Each one says "I am higher." It is not a matter of which is higher; in a sense, the cosmic consciousness or the universal essence, experiencing essence without an ego identity, is the other pole of non-existence, complete nothingness. The reality exists in two poles, existence and non-existence. Fullness that is love, and complete, utter emptiness or nothingness, are just the two poles of reality. Attachment to any of these is attachment. So the final attachment that must be resolved is the attachment to either existence or non-existence—God or nothing.

This resolution results in the big void, which eliminates identity itself—small or big, true or not true. There is no identity, no nothing to identify. There is no object whatsoever, even a boundless object. This big void, or complete nothingness, is most necessary for freedom because it eliminates attachment. It is the freedom beyond which there is no freedom. Of course, with that freedom, there will come everything. Everything will be freed—the cosmic consciousness, the guidance, the true identity, the personal essence—all essence in its various aspects will be there with no one experiencing it. It's just there. The cosmic existence is in the end seen as heaven, it is what is called heaven, even beyond heaven, the creator of heaven, God in some religions. We must see that attachment to naming either pole is simply attachment. Reality can be viewed either or both ways, or as the unity of the two.

To summarize, this process is a matter of investigating your identity, at any level of identification, and your attachments to it. That's why one of the most powerful techniques in spiritual traditions is to ask yourself, "Who am I?" and to keep asking. Every time you say, "That's me," investigate and continue asking, "Who am I?" until there is no one left to say it. It's not a matter of trying to push or do something. There's no need to do anything at all, all you need to do is understand what's there. The moment you want to do anything your motivation is attachment. The awareness of exactly what's there, whatever it is, without wanting or not wanting, is finally the void. So you can take this attitude from the beginning: simple awareness without ceasing is the understanding that leads to the final freedom. In fact, the means itself is the final freedom—bare objective awareness and understanding. All kinds of techniques exist to get to one or another of those levels, but the only technique, I believe, that will really bring the final freedom through all the levels is the technique of simply understanding, simply knowing, simple awareness. Any technique which involves doing something implies the existence of an identity who does it. It's all right to let your ego work for you; it can go far. But at some point it must go.

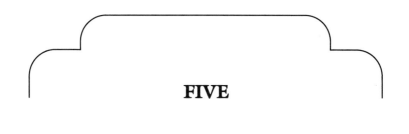

FIVE

The Teaching of No Hope

B y now, many of you have seen that we have a very effective, efficient method for teaching essential development and for achieving freedom. Many of you have had tastes and realizations of what this work is, and have seen that the teaching has a valid perspective. However, this is only one side of the teaching. Although there is a way through the teaching toward real freedom, that freedom will elude you, that happiness you believe you want will be out of your reach, as long as you desire it.

This is a dilemma. You come here, you work on your issues, you achieve some understanding, and you find that your efforts pay off. This gives you great hope, and strengthens your desire. Your desire gets even stronger:

"Oh, I really want my essence, I want to be free." But at every level, every stage of the work, that desire itself is what steps between you and freedom.

When I say there is a possibility for freedom, this does not mean you are necessarily going to achieve that freedom by wanting it more. When I say there is a teaching that leads to freedom, my intention is not to increase your desire for it. It is difficult for this not to happen. The more you see a method or a way that is effective, the more your hopes will rise, and the more your desire will be strengthened. Maybe the best method is an ineffective one, so that you give up from the beginning! Effective or powerful methods lead to more desire and hence, the freedom recedes even further.

So let's try to understand what I mean. Although it is difficult to see, this is the simplest and most basic truth about our mind: as long as you desire freedom, as long as you desire happiness, they will elude you.

"Well," somebody says, "what are we doing here? What are we supposed to do? If we want happiness and freedom, if we desire it and we're not going to have it, what are we doing here? After all, we are here because we want happiness and freedom."

Look at your experience right at this moment. At this very moment of your experience of yourself, what is happening? What do you see? You'll see there is an experience of what is happening, and another part of the experience that does not want what is happening. Am I right? That part of you which does not want what is happening wants something else, like freedom or happiness.

There is what is, and there is a part that says, "I want something other than what is." Doesn't that mean you're divided? Doesn't that mean you are in conflict with yourself? Doesn't that mean you're setting yourself against yourself? Part of your mind is opposing another part of your mind. That part of your mind opposing the other might be full of ideas and wonderful spiritual knowledge that says, "I want my essence. I want God and freedom." But, what is that part saying? Isn't it saying, "That other part of me is yucky; who wants it? I wish it would go to hell. I want to get away from it. I want to understand it so it will disappear."

This is what is called spiritual materialism, which is a dualistic, split perspective. There is a split in your mind, in yourself. There is what is there, and there is the part that doesn't like what is there, that wants something else. How are you going to arrive at harmony, integration, happiness, and freedom when there is a war inside you, when you are acting according to division and conflict? How can there be healing? How can there be harmony inside you when one part of you is against another part? Is it possible? Look at it logically. Look at your experience.

That is the simplest, most obvious, basic fact about every second of your experience. It doesn't matter what it is you want, whether you want to be richer, more beautiful, less scared, more enlightened, happier. As long as you want something that is not what is there, at that moment there is a division, a war. And, if you do your work according to that attitude of division, then, clearly, there will be more division. The war will continue.

It's like someone who says, "Well, the world is too full of wars. What can we do to stop the wars and have more peace? We'll strengthen our army, have more weapons, and that way we will have no more war." It's the same attitude which creates more division, more opposition, more war. How can you stop violence with violence? How can you stop the fight within you by going about it with fighting? You are strengthening the fighting part of you. You are strengthening the conflict. You are increasing the division.

It doesn't matter what it is you think you want at any given moment. It doesn't matter whether you think it's bad or good. That's not the point. The point here is the movement of the attitude of rejection, the attitude of wanting and desiring. The content is irrelevant. You might be experiencing misery and want happiness. You might be experiencing fear and want freedom. Or you might be experiencing freedom and feel afraid of losing it. You might be experiencing something wonderful and want to hold on to it, not want it to change.

It's all the same movement. There is a division in your experience, and there's a struggle. It's not peace. It's not harmony. It's not freedom. It is conflict and violence. I'm not saying anything esoteric. It is what you see if you just reflect on your experience.

If you have experienced your essence, or moments of freedom and release, you will see that in those moments of happiness—moments of being your essence—there is no judgment, no conflict, no wanting. Essence does not operate that way. Essence has no judgmental attitude at all, even towards personality. Essence is a presence, something that is there. It can be loving, compassionate, or any other quality, but it is not rejection of one thing and acceptance of another.

So this attitude of rejecting something which is there and wanting something else—which is the same movement—is actually the attitude of the personality itself. It is the personality, the ego personality. The basic structure of the personality is nothing but a rejection of what is there, and hope for something better.

In fact, the movement of rejection is what started the discord, the split between the personality and essence at the beginning when you were children. The personality began with this attitude. As a child you saw that one thing felt good and another felt bad. "I want what feels good. I don't want what feels bad." At some point you realized that there were good experiences and bad experiences. You developed an attitude toward what felt painful that you didn't want and what felt good that you did want. This is where the whole dynamic of fear and hope began. Fear is almost always simply the fear that something bad will happen. Hope is simply the hope that something pleasurable will happen. We can see that the process of the personality is basically a movement of fear and hope: fear of pain and hope for pleasure.

Fear and hope underlie the defensive mechanisms in the personality, the repression and resistance. What is resistance but resisting part of your experience? Resistance is ultimately rejection of something that you are experiencing. Resistance or defense is basically a rejection of part of you. Part of you is setting itself against another part and saying, "No, I don't want that." This attitude by itself creates division, conflict, and disharmony.

We see that the basic nature and movement of the personality is the movement of fear and hope and desire. Now you come here and you want to do the work. But how are you doing this? From that very perspective of rejection. "I'm going to do the work now, and use the Diamond Approach; I'm going to get my essence and get rid of my personality." Right? That's how you all think of it. "Now I'm going to get rid of my misery and have my essence which feels good." But that's how the whole dilemma started! That's the attitude which brought about the split between personality and essence! And now you want to get rid of that division by perpetuating it. You want to get rid of the conflict in yourself by completely identifying and engaging in that conflict!

Whenever you find yourself identified with a part of you opposing and fighting another part, you are being the ego personality. As you can see, it is quite hopeless to try to achieve freedom through rejection of any part of your experience. It is hopeless to try to get rid of something in order to gain freedom. There is no happiness in trying to attain happiness, because that very attitude of hope and rejection is itself the cause of the misery.

You don't need to accept or reject these ideas. Observe for yourself. Study and investigate it. Be aware of the movement, the attitude, the division. See how deep it goes in you. The more you experience essence, the clearer the division will be between what you feel is good and bad. The attitude of rejection can only make the conflict bigger.

I am not saying that this is a bad attitude. I'm saying that this attitude is the attitude of discord, of conflict, of suffering, of the personality. What does this mean? Are you now going to reject that attitude? "Ah, so that's what the problem is! Now I know what to do. I'll get rid of that attitude." Well, what are you doing then? Have you really listened?

You find yourself doing exactly the same thing. So what can be done? If you look at it closely, you'll see that the fact is that nothing can be done. The situation is completely and totally hopeless, and the sooner you realize that hopelessness, the better for you. When you see it is 100% hopeless, only then will you stop. Now you have some hope: "If I work harder and understand all this stuff about hopelessness, then things will change." But what are you saying? It's the same attitude. So nothing can be done about it. You can't get rid of it because the movement of wanting to get rid of it is, itself, the problem. You can't try to get something else because that is the same thing as rejecting what is there.

What we are talking about is not an academic issue. It is an issue at the very heart of each one of us all the time. It is always operating. Your mind is always engaged in it. If you look at your feelings, at your thoughts, your ideas, there is always this division. There is always a part that negates another part. There is always a movement of rejecting something and hoping for something new. Every thought you have, every feeling you have, every action you take is directed toward rejection or motivated by hope.

You are always perpetuating conflict, opposition and unhappiness. If you reject anything because you don't like it, you just compound the problem. So, are you starting to feel more hopeless? It is actually hopeless, and I'm not saying it just to scare you or make a joke. It's actually hopeless, and nothing can be done about it. The moment you want to do something, there it is, the rejection itself. It's very deep, very subtle. It operates on all levels and all places in your mind and in your being.

I'm talking about this today because there has been an attitude growing in this group as a result of the efficiency of this work, an attitude of acquisitiveness, an attitude of collecting, achieving, of attaining, which is exactly what we're talking about. Without the correct understanding, the work itself can backfire and start strengthening your personality instead of bringing freedom from the personality. At the present time, most of you are not able to disengage from the activity of attainment. And, as I've said, there is nothing you can do about it. It's hopeless. You find yourself engaged in it regardless of what happens.

Nothing can be done. There's no hope because the very attitude of hope, the very attitude of doing something, is a rejection, is itself strengthening the personality, which is the attitude of conflict. I'm saying all of this, but at the same time we do have work here. We do have a group and I do work with people. What am I saying then? Am I contradicting myself? If nothing can be done, if the situation is completely hopeless, then what's the point of having a school, what's the point of the teaching, what's the point of the work? Are you wasting your time, your money, your effort?

It's a paradoxical situation, that the situation is completely hopeless, nothing can be done, and yet at the same time there is a school where you can work to bring about freedom. This situation can be understood. The understanding is that the school and the teaching exist, not so you'll strengthen your hope, but so that in time, you will see that what I'm saying is true. The school is useful only for finally bringing about the perception and the certain understanding that it is hopeless. That is the function of the teaching. Only when you completely understand from your own observation of your mind and reality that it is hopeless, only then will you give up. When there's complete hopelessness and you give up, not out of despair, but out of understanding, then the freedom will be there. The freedom will not come as a result of your achieving anything. The freedom will arise only as a result of understanding the situation. In fact, the freedom is not a result of understanding the situation, the freedom is the understanding of the situation.

There is hope, but the hope is that we find out finally that there is no hope. When you see from your own experience, that there's no hope for you to bring about your freedom, then you will stop the struggle. Only then will you be willing to say, "Okay, there's nothing I can do; I'd better stop this business." When you are not engaged in the hope, in the rejection, then there's no opposition and no conflict. There is harmony, happiness and freedom. This is the birth of love.

As you can see, it's very tricky. Right away everyone will say, "Oh good, now I'll work hard at getting to that understanding." Why? What are you motivated by when you think that way? What I want to do is help you see the hopelessness of the situation, but the mind still grasps at hope. "Ah, there's a chance here after all. There's no chance the other way." The mind can't do anything else. Its function is to hope or reject. If it doesn't do one or the other, it will completely stop. What's left? What's left if we understand? There is what is there at any second. What is there is actually there whether you like it or not. Rejecting it doesn't make it go away. You only separate it from yourself and create discord. Hoping for something else doesn't make what's there go away. You might suppress it, deny it, or repress it, but this only creates discord, conflict, and suffering. Remember that we are discussing here your inner experience. Don't confuse yourself by trying to apply this teaching to action in the world before you understand your mind.

The only thing you can do is accept unconditionally what is. What's left is an unconditional awareness of what is there, an unconditional and motiveless understanding of the truth of the situation.

This is the attitude of essence, of reality, and not of the personality. That is the hope, but it is the hope that cannot be felt as hope. There is no goal in it, no division or struggle in it. There is the pure, motiveless, love of the truth, which is what is there.

If you love truth for its own sake, the truth will free you. But if you hope the truth will free you, you cannot be free. You must love the truth for its own sake, without hope. Then there's no question of freedom/no freedom, no question of essence/no essence, no question of enlightenment/no enlightenment. It's just love of truth, and that's it. Nothing else is there. Anything else will bring discord. Accepting what is, understanding what is there, loving the truth that is happening at every second is the natural state, the state without personality, the state of no-mind, is the state of no-division. It is the state of hanging loose.

When I tell you to love the truth, to love what is there, to accept completely what is there without any conditions, what does that mean? What is there at this very moment may be a rejection of what is there. Are you going to reject that rejection? It's a subtle process to pay attention, and to be aware of that movement. The complete awareness of this movement will bring about understanding, which, as we have said, *is* the freedom. The truth of the situation is the freedom. Awareness does not need to be motivated. It is what is there. We're always aware of something. As long as there is motivation for anything, awareness is restricted away from one thing and toward another. When there is no motivation, awareness will just be there, free. With awareness, there is a possibility of understanding, of seeing the truth. Because awareness and understanding are possible, freedom and happiness are possible.

The correct perspective from which you can do this work is always to be aware of whether you are interested in the truth of what is happening right now, or whether you are trying to achieve something. Are you doing the work now to acquire something, to arrive at a certain goal, or are you doing it because you love the truth?

This is a shift in attitude that is needed for us to finally understand the hopelessness of the situation. You are caught and divided because you still have hope that things will be different. That hope creates desire, that desire creates rejection of what is there, the rejection of what is there creates division, the division creates conflict, the conflict creates suffering, the suffering then creates searching. The searching creates more rejection and more conflict and the cycle continues.

You may think I'm saying that there's no point to the work. There is a point: to make it possible for us to understand the situation. Essence is needed because essence is what will help you accept what is there. Many other methods try to understand the situation without the presence of essence, which makes it very difficult. Here it is easy for us to realize and experience essence. Essence is there not so that we will gain some pleasure, or satisfy our desires, or get something. Essence is there so that we learn in time that truth is what matters.

If you reject the truth, there is conflict and suffering. That is a basic truth. There is nothing else. It doesn't matter what is there, whether it's essence, personality, mind, body. It doesn't matter at all, really.

If you reject it, you reject it. If you accept it, you accept it. If you reject your experience, you take the side of suffering. If you accept your experience, you take the side of essence. That's how it is. It's not a matter of what you get, or what you have. It's where you come from, your attitude. Do you operate from personality or from essence? That's the real transformation.

We must understand here that when I speak of acceptance, I'm not referring to an active attitude, holding on to or being attached to something. I mean merely being there with the experience, without judgment. It is presence with openness to whatever is manifesting in your consciousness.

You can accumulate experiences of essence and have mountains of it, but if you have an attitude of acquisition, of achievement, of reaching some goal, then you are increasing your personality; it's just getting bigger.

There is bound to be suffering. There's no other way. But it's possible to be free from suffering when there is no desire to be free from suffering. There is a possibility of freedom, but it will happen only when there is no desire for freedom. Ultimately we need to drop the desire for freedom.

This doesn't mean you can now go about eliminating your desires. What you can do is understand the movement of desire. If you look at yourself in your meditation you'll see that your mind is moving around, your emotions are moving around. When you're angry, what are you angry about? You're angry because what's happening is not what you want to happen. You don't like what's happening. Somebody does something you don't like, or you experience something you don't like. Ultimately, anger is based on rejection. When you're sad, why are you sad? You are sad because you lost something, or because something is not happening the way you want it to happen, or something you want is not there. So sadness is based on rejection. All emotions are based on the rejection of what is now, and your thoughts are the same way. Complete freedom means no personality at all. Complete freedom means essence—no mind and no emotions.

This doesn't mean you should reject your sadness and anger. We're trying to understand things. We're not trying to get anywhere. The work is not about getting freedom or happiness. The work is not there to get rid of your suffering. The work is there to help you see things as they are. The work is there to help you finally realize how things actually are. The work is there so that, in time, you'll be aligned with truth, you'll be on the side of reality.

When you are aligned with reality, there's no concern about whether there's pain or no pain. Reality is what is there right at this moment. The truth is understanding and accepting reality. An unconditional understanding of that reality is the only possible sane attitude that a person can take. And ultimately, it is not an action or an attitude at all. It is simply the truth.

When you see the movement of your emotions as rejection of the present and desire for something else, when you see the movement of your thoughts as a feverish activity to experience something, to get something, to hope for something, to imagine something that is better than now, you'll see that the feelings will stop, the thoughts will become quiet, and there will be complete emptiness. The emptiness, then, is the absence of all personality. Then it is possible for essence to be there in the most real way, in the only real way.

This can happen only through understanding, only through the truth, and through nothing else. Understanding is simply understanding, not an achievement of understanding. Understanding means seeing exactly what is there. It is the action of selfless love. You can't see what is there if you are rejecting what is there. You can begin by understanding your rejection of what is there.

As you see, this work is not a matter of being better or worse, more or less. It is not a matter of getting your essence, or of achieving enlightenment or freedom. All these are ultimately concepts. The real truth is there, existing as it is, without your mind saying what is good or bad. It is being present with what is there.

Any rejection of what is there is suffering, even if that rejection is predicated on the hope of reaching God or freedom or enlightenment. Enlightenment or freedom will come as a result of doing this work, but that is not the issue. The issue is not enlightenment. The issue is not freedom. The issue is "what is."

If you experience certain essential aspects such as freedom or some kind of consciousness, and you want to hold on to it, work for it, what are you doing then?

The factual truth, then, is the truth of "no hope." The ultimate truth is "what is." If there is any desire, there is a rejection of what is. If there is any wanting, there is a rejection of what is. This is how the personality started and is perpetuated: by a rejection of what is and by creating a division.

The personality is a point of view. Enlightenment, or reality, is also a point of view—nothing else. It is not a

certain state. Personality is the point of view that there is
something we need to get, somewhere we need to go.
Enlightenment or freedom or reality is a point of view,
that "what is" is what is. That is what is there and there is
no hope for anything else.

When I say, "accepting what is," I do not mean accepting unconsciousness in yourself. Accepting what is means
complete consciousness, means complete awareness of
what is. When one is unconscious of what is, there is a
rejection of what is. The enlightened point of view, or the
natural point of view, which is what I prefer to call it, is
that there is what is, all the time. It can be personality,
essence, heat or cold. "What is" is what is. Very simple. If
there is any attempt to get something else, to change
what is there in your inner experience, then there is conflict. It is a certain understanding, which is simply the
perception of how things work. It is not getting anything, not trying to go somewhere. It is just the perception of how things actually operate.

All the work is needed in all its levels, all its aspects.
Essence is needed in all its aspects for us in time to be able
to tolerate seeing and accepting what is there. But there is
no point in starting at the wrong end. Why not start from
the correct perspective at the beginning so there will be
fewer illusions, less resistance, less discord, and so that
there will be the attitude of sincerely exploring truth?

When you take the attitude of truth, you will understand that pain and suffering will increase for a while
because what you've been rejecting will start manifesting. This will happen until you understand it. Then
things will change.

Things will change, but the change will be slower if
you are invested in the change. Change will be facilitated
if your interest is in the truth. Truth is nothing mysterious. Truth is always what is there, your experience at that

moment, not in the past and not in the future. The truth is now, and your life is now.

Do you ever actually live in the past? Do you ever actually live in the future? Your life is what is now. Your mind might be going toward the past or the future, but "what is" is what is now. The verb "is" means being—right now, at this very second. So, there is life only in what is. Anything else is just imagination.

Now we'll have questions.

Student: Is hope an essential quality?

A.H. Almaas: Hope is not an essential quality. The way you experience it, hope is a rejection of the present. Essence is the hope. Essence is the hope in the sense that essence allows you to see the perspective of hopelessness. Essence is the hope in the sense that it will show you that the attitude of your personality is hopeless. That's the objective hope. But the feeling of hope is future oriented.

When you're feeling hopeful, what are you doing? Aren't you rejecting what is there? Don't you want something else? How can that be essence? Essence is being, right now. Essence is the hope in that it will resolve the hopelessness of the situation. But essence is not a feeling of hope.

S: I'm afraid I won't be able to function if I give up hoping. How will I be motivated to do anything?

AH: That's understandable. I was working with someone recently and after a while she got into the space of no mind, no thoughts, no hope, nothing. She didn't know what she was going to do. She was a little scared. "How am I going to drive my car?" And she didn't know what she was going to do because she had no motivation to do anything. But, at the end of the session, she said, "Where's the bathroom?" She didn't need her mind to be functioning in order to know she wanted to use the bathroom. If you're hungry, you get something to eat. If you're tired, you sleep. If you need to use the bathroom, you'll know it. It's not a question of desire or hope. When hopefulness ceases, essence begins to flow and functioning becomes the motiveless flow of selfless love.

In essence, there is a movement towards what is good, but what is good is now, and the movement of essence is towards the now. It is not towards something else in the future. You might experience it as a movement in the future because that's how your mind functions. However, the greater the presence of essence, the more you are in the now. Essence is presence so it can only be in the now.

Your mind can function only according to what happened to you in the past; but "what is" has nothing to do with what happened in the past. What is is what is. But you want to condition "what is" according to what was. Who says what happened in the past is supposed to happen again, or is not supposed to happen again? Who are you to tell?

S: Could you say more about separating effort and desire?

AH: Effort and desire go together. Effort is based on desire. If there is no desire for something, why will there be effort? First there is a rejection of what is now and a hope of something else. That hope creates a desire. Desire hooks into the will. Then the will to accomplish the desire is used by the personality. Will in the service of the personality is effort.

I'm not saying desires are bad and you shouldn't have them. There is no judgment in what I'm saying. I'm saying that understanding is the point of view of reality. Effort is always based on rejection, isn't it? Effort is always aimed at getting somewhere.

At the beginning you use effort, and that is fine. You will continue using effort until you understand at some point that effort is a problem. You'll see that it's not a matter of stopping the effort. You cannot stop effort and you cannot stop desire. If you want to stop effort or desire, what are you doing? You're engaging in the personality's point of view. The only thing you can do is to understand the movement of effort. What we're doing here is activating a flame, a flame which loves the truth. I'm not interested in teaching you to reject something or accept something else. There is a possibility of a certain perception, a certain way of living that is not based on anything in the personality—not on desire, effort, conflict, hope, search, past, future, any of that—but is a purely motiveless interest in the truth.

That motiveless interest in the truth can be quite a relief. Imagine nothing to do, nowhere to go, nothing to achieve. Imagine yourself sitting sometime with nowhere to get to, no enlightenment to achieve, nothing to get rid of. Isn't that a carefree attitude? That's how we were when we were kids. We didn't think we had a personality to get rid of. We had no idea that there was something like enlightenment or essence. We just did what we did and that was it. That's the natural state, the state of innocence.

What I'm saying now does not apply only to the work; it applies to everything, to every desire, to anything, any part of your life. For example, when you're in bed with your lover, if there's an effort to have pleasure, there is no pleasure. If there is a desire for pleasure, then that by itself will reduce the pleasure. There is only what is at any second, not just when you are doing the work, but when you are driving your car, making a sale, talking to your friend, taking a shit, eating, going to sleep, washing your face, brushing your teeth, punching somebody, it's always the same.

At some point all of that becomes channeled, concentrated and focused on the work. All desire, all efforts, all hoping, all seeking become one desire, one hope, one seeking, and that is the work.

S: Could you say more about desire and fear?

AH: We know fear in terms of an emotion, but if you look at it closely, you will see that fear is really based on an attitude of conflict. Fear exists as long as you want something and don't want something else. If you want something, then you're afraid you won't get it. If you don't want something, you're afraid you will get it. Fear is the same thing as desire. Fear and desire are two ends of the same stick. If you are afraid of being hurt, then you desire not to be hurt. If you are afraid you're going to be rejected, then you desire acceptance. So fear is like desire, based on a rejection of what is now. And that goes through all the levels, all the way. Some parts are difficult to see, like fear of death and things like that, but still it's the same. Fear of death is ultimately fear of life, or desire for it.

If you fear the truth, you are afraid things will happen in a way that you don't want them to happen. You're afraid if you see the truth, you will feel pain. There is a judgment of pain. There is a rejection of the truth at that very moment because of fear of the pain. If there is fear of truth, it does not need to be rejected, it needs to be understood.

What I am saying is something to be investigated. You do not need to accept it on faith. See for yourself.

I want to expose the attitude of acquisitiveness, greed, accumulation that has been happening in some people in this group. The attitude of coming to the work wanting something, thinking you're going to get something, will only bring about more discord. If you come here because you are interested in understanding, in seeing the truth of how things are, you will not create division in yourself.

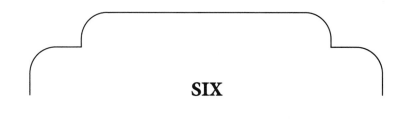

SIX

Acceptance

We can look at our situation in terms of rejection and acceptance. The personality can do only one thing: it can only say "no." If you look at the movement and the actions of your personality you will observe that there is basically a rejection of your own experience. The personality's main function is to say "no" to your sensations, feelings, perceptions, and experience. It can do other things, such as act in the world and so on. But if we look at what it does in your relationship with yourself it is mainly rejecting, and even when it seems to be saying "yes" it says "no." Even when the personality is saying "yes" to something in you, it is usually saying "no" to something else in the same breath. You can see this happening minute by minute; it is not something that happens once in a while. Without the "no," the personality would not exist as we know it.

The basic movement of what we call ourselves or our personality is desire for something different, and that desire makes us effort toward fulfilling it. But that hope and that desire and that effort are all a rejection of what is there. They are all a rejection of the present, of reality. They say "no" to what exists at that moment. This is the constant movement of personality, no matter what the activity is: working on a job, doing a task, sensing yourself, having sex, eating food, driving your car. All imply desire along with a rejection of what we are at the moment. So we see that the personality doesn't know how to act without rejection. Any preference, every preference of one thing you experience over another is a rejection of something you experience. When you say "no" to a part of you, isn't one part of you setting itself against another part and saying "I don't want it"? So rejection creates division and conflict in you. That conflict creates resistances, blocks, and defenses. You don't want to feel the conflict so you don't feel as much, you cover it up, defend against it, resist it. Then you don't like that either so you reject the rejection; in trying to move away from the conflict more conflict is created. This is a vicious cycle of rejection, division, conflict, discord. There is a war, in a sense, going on within us.

When we see these conflicts and rejections, what do we do? Usually we can't help but try to get rid of the conflict, which is more rejection. At each moment there is either a "yes" or a "no," nothing in between. It doesn't matter what it is you're rejecting. Even if you are rejecting rejection, it's still the same thing, rejection. We are not saying this so you'll be hard on yourself but to understand the situation. First we need to see that the basic movement of our mind, of personality, is a rejection, mainly self-rejection. One might reject other people or circumstances, but it's mainly a rejection of oneself, a part of oneself.

What makes us do that? One way of seeing it is that your internal critic, your superego is rejecting your experience. We have learned that the superego comes from identifications with our parents, especially our parents' superegos. We might say we took on rejection from our parents. My father didn't like me when I was angry, so now I reject my anger. My mother didn't like me when I wanted her, so now I reject my wanting. Thus one of the ways that an attitude of rejection develops is through identification with the rejecting attitude of the environment in early childhood. This is why early in our work we learn how to defend against the superego. At the beginning, and for a long time, we need to defend against the superego so that we are able to experience ourselves more objectively. We need to defend from superego attacks and judgments not only because the attacks are painful but more importantly to be able to look at what's there. If you are in a battle, it's hard to pay attention to the subtleties of your consciousness. When no one is attacking you, you might let yourself more freely explore your experience.

Actually, the attitude of rejection is a much deeper and more primitive mechanism than just the identification with the parents. There is something that precedes the identification with the parents. It is already there before you identify with the parents, before you even know there are parents. It is one of the earliest movements in the organism. It happens, in the first few months of life, when the baby still isn't even aware that he is separate from the parent. Let's look at the experience of a very young baby. When the baby is not asleep or content he will experience some kind of disturbance: gas, full bowels, full bladder, hunger, cold, etc. If the bowels are full, automatically there is an elimination of the contents. If the bladder is full, just relaxing lets it flow out. If the baby is hungry, it cries and the mother puts food in its mouth and everything returns to normal. This movement is called a charge and discharge cycle. There is a tension that creates a charge, an increase of energy and activity, which is released through the defecation, the feeding, the comforting; this is the discharge. The child returns to the contented, relaxed, peaceful state. In this cycle there is not yet an action of rejection. It is the organism spontaneously contracting and expanding, charging and discharging. It is a natural movement to bring about the state of rest and relaxation. The mother helps the child in this regulation because the child is still unable to feed and take care of itself.

If everything continues in this way, under the best and most balanced circumstances, the child will grow up to do for itself what its mother did. When there is a disturbance the child can take care of it naturally without even thinking about discharging it. This is what we call autonomic regulation. Hungry, you eat; tired, you go to sleep; bladder's full, go to the bathroom. So, the rejection isn't there. If that happens consistently, then the child grows up to be an adult who can do these things naturally and spontaneously. Then there is no neurosis, no conflict, and the personality will not have an attitude of rejection and defensiveness.

However, for many reasons, things don't generally go that well. Sometimes the child has gas or pain and the mother doesn't come in time, so the pain or tension is not released. The baby is still dependent on the mother and the environment to help release these charges or tensions. Sometimes it is not that the mother isn't there, but that the baby gets sick or constipated or can't keep food down. Then there is pain that is not discharged when it needs to be. Things are in fact much worse than that; if this were the whole story, it would be wonderful. However, the truth is that the baby usually lives in an environment in which the parents are not the most wonderful beings on earth. The child is very open, and can feel the pain and suffering going on in its immediate environment. The child is aware of its own body and can also feel the tension, rigidity, and pain in the mother's body or anyone else it is with. If the parents are suffering, the child feels it. If the mother is suffering, the baby suffers too. The pain never gets discharged. We are not even considering the acts of cruelty that so many babies endure. Some parents take their own conflicts out on the child in physical abuse, neglect, or emotional rejection. All these things affect the child in the same negative way—there remains pain that is not discharged. So the natural movement is impeded, and the child doesn't return to its natural harmony. There might be difficulty in the body of the child. Sometimes even when the mother acts in a loving way toward the baby she is feeling anguish, or self-rejection, or other negative feelings inside herself. The baby always feels this pain, and the mother isn't discharging it for herself or the baby.

At the beginning, there is an innate confidence that there will be a discharge. It is like an instinct; it does not need to be learned. This innate confidence is like the contraction and expansion of an amoeba, which just releases itself. There is no hope or desire or fear. If the environment is supportive and the body is normal, then that confidence is not disturbed and the child grows up with it. If the mother is loving and responds when the baby needs help then that confidence is supported.

There is, then, a state of innocence at the beginning. When the organism functions harmoniously and is supported in doing so, this innocence develops into an innate confidence. It becomes an implicit basic trust in the universe.

But what happens when the tensions don't get discharged? What happens to that confidence in who we are, in our organism, in the functioning of our system, in our environment? Our trust and confidence become eroded little by little, or it does not have the chance to emerge and develop. It happens very early, usually during the first few months, because the disturbances in the baby's body and the pain in the mother are there all the time. The innate innocence, that the child is born with and that can become trust, begins to be lost. The organism does not develop the confidence that it can regulate itself, that things will happen the way they should. There is no longer confidence that the harmony will remain, because the child feels pain and it doesn't go away. And what does the child do to get rid of its pain, when it doesn't just naturally get discharged?

First of all, there will be an awareness, an increasing awareness that there are things that are painful. If they remain, there is a fixation of the organism, the mind, on those painful things. Then, those are differentiated from and contrasted with the good feelings we have at other times. Before the undischarged pain happened, there was no need for the differentiation. Only when things are not being smoothly regulated does the child begin to notice that this is painful and this is pleasurable. A differentiation arises in the mind, which increases the more there is pain, suffering and frustration. And when the child also sees that the pain isn't eliminated, it becomes afraid for its existence. If the pain and frustration continue, the child cannot tolerate it. Its system is not mature enough to tolerate the frustration or to discharge it by itself. If the pain and the frustration continue, they will have a disintegrating effect on the organism, and the child will begin to experience organismic fear for its very survival. The presence of the frustration and pain changes the innocence not into confidence and trust but into fear and distrust.

Now the child must learn to deal with this situation. The organism must adapt to the continual disturbance of its functioning because if the autonomic regulation doesn't function well there will be a disruption in the nervous system and in the body as a whole. So the child turns to a very primitive mechanism that the body has in order to deal with noxious things. We see this first defense mechanism when the child has eaten something it cannot digest and it throws it up. Vomiting, spitting out is a rejection. That's what the child finds he can do, spit it out, reject it. As you can see, this is not the same thing as defecation. Defecation is the end of a process, getting rid of what's left over from the natural process of digestion. Throwing up implies that something is wrong in the natural flow downwards, something is not assimilable in the digestion so it does not complete the natural course. The child throws up things that come from the outside, the sour milk or whatever food the child cannot handle. However, the child at that time has no conception of inside and outside, so when there is any pain or disturbance he will try to throw it up, spit it out.

How does a child throw up bad feelings or frustration that he cannot deal with and that he fears will destroy him? The first defense mechanism is an extension of the body's defense of spitting out; it is projection. The child tries to believe it is not in him, it is outside. He tries to pretend to himself that he isn't feeling bad, it is that Mommy is terrible. It may be true that the mother is in pain or is frustrating or hurting the child, but it is also true that the child is feeling bad. The negativity is both inside and outside, it's still non-differentiated, there is no true separation from mother yet.

How can the child project out its feelings? To project we have to believe that emotionally there is an inside and outside. For me to believe this feeling is not mine, that it's coming from outside so that it won't have a disintegrating effect on me, I must believe that I am separate from the outside. The mechanism of projection necessitates the erection of boundaries around oneself, which result in the sense that we are separate from our environment. Projection and the erection of boundaries happen at the same time, and are interdependent.

This then is the process through which we split ourselves off from a sense of unity with everything, which is the perspective of the true self, our essence. The truth is that experientially there are no boundaries, I am not separate from anything else. And energetically, I am not bound by my body. My body can eject food, but emotionally I can't actually spit out my emotions and frustrations. So first there is a projection which necessitates the erection of boundaries, of separateness from the energetic field, from all existence. But in order for the child to project successfully, to feel that this feeling isn't his, he has to stop feeling it. This means he must dull the feelings, or repress them or split them off. In order to project, we must suppress something in ourselves, we have to not feel a part of us. The projection and the dullness, suppression or splitting off of our feelings and sensations constitute the rejection which is modeled on the spitting-out mechanism. This rejection, of course, creates disharmony.

As you see, the attitude of rejection happens very early, usually within the first few weeks or months of life. There is an organismic necessity for this attitude because of the imperfect environment. The child is trying to reject his pain, suffering, and contraction. On that base of rejection of pain is built all the identification that comes from the parents and becomes the superego. The superego's attitude of rejection and putting oneself down and humiliation is basically the same as when you have food and say, "Yuck, I don't like it." The superego says, "Yuck, you shouldn't be like that." Later on, anal rejection is incorporated.

Personality is nothing but a boundary that separates us from other people so that we can protect ourselves from what we think is noxious to us. But when you block part of yourself, you create tensions and armoring in the body. Not only do you have a pain that cannot be discharged, now you're suppressing it, or pushing it away. This creates an increasing tension which in turn makes your capacity for healthy regulation and discharge even less. So the situation gets worse. The child had to suppress his feelings because he had no other way to discharge the pain and negative feelings. However, gradually the healthy cycle of charge and discharge that we call autonomic regulation, the spontaneous contraction and expansion that keeps us vital, strong, and alive becomes eroded, and the trust and confidence do not develop as innocence is lost. We become increasingly dependent on external agents to release our tensions, which gives even more power to the rejecting attitude of the superego—"If I'm good enough my mother will love me and help me discharge." When you were dependent on her, it was true that if there had been enough love, enough acceptance, enough support it wouldn't have been so bad. But we grow up always wanting that love and support, and have no confidence that we can do it for ourselves.

Then we proceed to project mother onto others, and try to get their approval so they will love us and help us. That is one of the main motivations for sex, for example. Sex is a physical discharge. We charge up and then discharge; so sex mostly becomes an attempt to discharge our tensions and pain. We can see how deep the motivation for sex is, rooted in the beginning stages of life. It is like wanting your mother to come and feed you and make you feel wonderful, or wanting her to help you spit up your milk. By now you have no confidence that you can do it yourself because of all your blockage. So, it's always, "If I can just find Prince/Princess Charming, then I can discharge all my tensions and everything will be fine." In most relationships, the other person is someone to make you feel good. If they make you feel good, you love them. If they make you feel bad, you reject them. Usually we want the other person to regulate us. When you build up tension, you say, "I love you, let's make love." It doesn't mean that sex can't have other motivations like true love and appreciation, but most often there is a compulsion from accumulated tension and a desire for discharge.

Now that we know what the situation is, and how it started, how do we go about dealing with it? How can we regain our original innocence and develop the ability to discharge? How can we enhance our confidence and our capacity for self-regulation? As we have seen, rejecting our experience makes it worse. True, the child needed to do it for a time, but if it continues, more and more tension accumulates, and the capacity for regulation decreases until the child becomes neurotic. If we can regain the capacity to spontaneously charge and discharge, if we can change the rejection pattern and reconnect with our natural confidence and trust, we call that self-realization. Obviously everyone longs to regain that harmony and relaxation.

So how can we learn to accept our experience? First, we need to know that we do not know how to accept our experience. Personality doesn't know how to accept. Ego personality began as a rejection and that is what it knows. Even the presence of personality is rejection, it is saying "no" to your being. What you think is you, your personality, is covering up your truth even when you are not actively rejecting your experience. Personality came into being in order to cover up the real experience, to avoid pain and frustration. The personality is a "no"; it can't say "yes."

So how can we learn to accept? When you say, "I should learn to accept my anger," aren't you rejecting your rejection of your anger? Aren't you rejecting the resistance? If you have a desire to be free from the personality, isn't that a rejection of the personality? The personality doesn't know how to do it. Most people have decided that it is hopeless, and it is hopeless for the personality to do it.

However, hopelessness is based on hopefulness, and hence on rejection. The understanding of no hope is not the same as hopelessness and despair. It is based on objective truth.

But if we look back to the beginning of the rejection, what was it we rejected? What we rejected was pain and suffering. First we said, "I don't want to feel this, it hurts, it's dangerous," but over time it became, "I don't want to feel this because I want something better, I want to improve myself, to succeed." We even believe the rejection is a kindness toward ourselves.

Whatever you think of doing—becoming successful, becoming lovable, getting enlightened, realized—the moment you're thinking of changing yourself, you are rejecting yourself. Whenever you want to change what you're feeling, you're rejecting your experience. You want to spit yourself out.

What we can do essentially, is not to try to say "yes," because trying to say "yes" is a rejection. What we can do is just see how we are rejecting. In the beginning the rejection was an attempt to get rid of the pain, but we didn't get rid of it, we simply stopped seeing it. We weren't able to throw it up or otherwise discharge it, so we numbed our sensitivity. Now we can allow ourselves to be sensitive, to experience without judgment, without saying a "no," without saying "I'm seeing it so that it will go away." We can do this when we are interested in the truth for its own sake: to see, to be aware, to be conscious, to be with, and to feel what is there in your experience with no rejection, what is now. It gets very subtle; it is difficult not to reject your experience. When you sit to meditate, why are you meditating? You cannot help but do it because you want to reject yourself; this is a fact and it too needs to be allowed. Don't tell yourself, "No, I'm really accepting it." Admit the truth, that you are sitting because you want to be different. Just be aware of the rejection.

Meditation can be seen as nothing but the spontaneous and passive awareness of the movement of rejection and desire. The awareness of the rejection is the meditation. You can be aware of this truth all the time; in fact meditation is actually needed all the time. Meditation is awareness of the truth, so we sense, look, and listen all the time to be aware of the simple truth of what is now. If you want anything else, it is a rejection. If you do anything beyond the awareness and the understanding, there is rejection, and then you're compounding the problem. We can only see the truth, we can only understand. If we see the movement of the mind, we will realize that even our understanding, even our awareness at the beginning is motivated by desire, hope and rejection. It cannot be helped. But what we can do is to be aware of that, and not pretend otherwise.

The whole thing is to see the truth, admit the truth, because at the beginning the rejection was nothing but the rejection of the truth, of what was there. Rejection of yourself is a rejection of your experience. So we work on paying attention to seeing what is there, which in the beginning and for a long while always includes rejection. We see how we cannot but reject. If we look at what the rejection does to us, we see the hate and hostility in it, we see that we are being hurt. In time, understanding the truth of the situation will lessen the rejection.

Accepting means not rejecting. The personality can reject or it can stop rejecting. This simply means that the personality isn't doing anything; it's not active at that moment. When we see the movement of rejection and feel what it does to us, compassion will emerge. You will see yourself as if you are seeing a little child or a baby being rejected. The more you perceive this rejection, the more you will experience love for yourself. If you see that movement of rejection without trying to stop it, since stopping is engaging in that movement, the more you disengage from the movement of rejection. The more you see, the more you disengage, which allows space for something else to emerge. As this process continues, the disidentification and disengagement from the movement of rejection becomes complete. Then acceptance will come.

Acceptance will not be the personality accepting. Acceptance will be essence coming; it will be like a benediction, a blessing, a gentle rain. The personality cannot accept. It can surrender to the truth of the moment— which is the same as the stopping of rejection—surrender and allow what is there to be there without preference and judgment. For example, if you feel your knee now, you have no judgment, good or bad, about it; this is the attitude of allowing. When that surrender to the truth happens, then the acceptance comes and is experienced as a gentle, cool shower. After the hot harshness of the constant rejection of the personality it feels so cool and refreshing. Your heart will be cool and your mind rested. The feverish movement of rejection is gone. You cannot act in such a way as to accept, but you can allow

acceptance by allowing and perceiving the rejection. Even
the lack of awareness of a feeling is a rejection of it.
Dullness, dimness, numbing all are rooted in rejection.
Often the personality pretends to accept things as they
are, in order to avoid a feeling. When you're completely
aware of what is happening and not doing anything about
it, you surrender to the truth and open the door for
acceptance to rain on you. It washes away the pain that
you wanted to avoid and reject. You don't want to reject
the pains, you are aware and surrender to their existence.

Essence is acceptance, not as approval but as a healing
agent. It is the spontaneous inner charge and discharge;
the cleansing without rejection. When the personality
stops because it sees that its activity is painful, it stops
through understanding, and not through rejection. In
fact, it is not that the personality stops and acceptance
comes; they happen at the same time. The letting go of
the personality and the washing of essence are the same
process. Your personality and essence have the same
understanding at that moment so they operate together;
personality is not rejected but understood with compassion and love. Acceptance is actually an aspect of essence;
it is not an activity.

Our work is to see the truth. It is to be in harmony
with the truth, to be steadfast in the truth. Ultimately
you will regain your trust and confidence in the truth.
That confidence is regained just by seeing the truth; that
is a miracle by itself. It becomes as implicit as it was when
you were a trusting infant.

When we allow what is there in our experience we are
not rejecting the pain as we did when we were babies. It
can become like it was before the pain and rejection, when
you were a very young baby and were confident that when
the pain came it would go away at some time. Even more
than this: it is the regaining of original innocence through

the development of confidence and basic trust. It is a return to the natural process: I eat, my belly is full, I digest the food, I shit it out. There is no desire, no hope, no rejection; the feelings and sensations come, they are experienced and assimilated, and what's left over is discharged, washed away. Then there is spontaneity.

Our work is learning how to be in the truth, how to surrender to the truth. You see, although we see acceptance in terms of washing away of tensions, which is a washing away of the personality contractions, it must begin with accepting the truth of those very contractions. So the attitude of complete acceptance and complete perception of the truth coincide. You cannot understand an experience if you are rejecting it, or rejecting part of it.

No rejection means no comparative judgment of one thing over another. You don't say, "I like my essence, but I don't like my personality." Who is saying that and what does that mean? It is rejection of the attitude of essence itself. Essence just lets things be. Only when we allow ourselves to see the movement of rejection and allow our understanding to unfold completely does the simultaneous cessation of the movement of rejection and the flow of acceptance happen. Then we regain our confidence and trust in our organism, which is actually a trust in the truth.

Seeing and understanding the truth allows this development, because when you completely see the workings of rejection you will feel the suffering and see that our usual way of life doesn't work, it causes suffering. You began the rejection because you didn't want suffering, and it's natural that you want to be happy. The point is not that you should like pain or dislike pleasure; the point is to really understand that the way we go about trying to be happy creates pain. When you see that you will eventually stop. When you completely see your rejection, hope, and desire, you can bring to awareness the pain that you are rejecting and stay with it, because it is your truth in the moment.

If you are attached to something, you are rejecting the possibility of it not being there. If you are attached to a person, you are rejecting the absence of that person. There is a holding on, which is a rejection of openness to experience.

An attitude of being steadfast in the truth, an attitude of non-rejection, does not require taking any action. It is not seeing attachment and trying to get rid of it, it is not a matter of getting somewhere. If you simply accept what is, release and freedom will follow. In the attitude of acceptance itself, there is no desire even for freedom. If you feel hope, then your hope is simply a part of the rejection that needs to be seen.

When the confidence in ourselves and our organism is implicit there is everlasting happiness. We aren't trying to be confident or self-conscious about it. We don't have to feel confident about ordinary functions like walking; we know our feet will take us where we want to go without hoping that we will get there. We know we can do it. That is the kind of confidence we are talking about, the kind of confidence that can happen in our consciousness when there is complete acceptance.

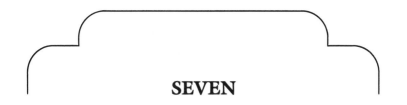

SEVEN

Change and Truth

T his work is for you to learn to know yourself, to pay attention to yourself, to be watchful of your feelings, attitudes, and thoughts. Observe what your attitude is toward what's happening inside and outside, to yourself and to others and to the situation. What are you doing with yourself? What is the movement, the action happening within you? What is the commentary? What is the reaction to what is happening inside you and outside you? Be watchful of that, be aware of it now. What are you saying to yourself, what are you wanting to do about what's happening? Are you saying, "Oh, this is good" or are you saying, "Well, I don't know about this, I'd like it to be different." What is your attitude toward yourself, toward your feeling, your thinking? Is it okay to have the experience that you are having? Is it completely okay? Or is part of it okay and part of it not okay? Is it okay for it to be the way it is, or should it be different? And if it's not okay for it to be this way, how do you want it to be? If you're looking at what's happening inside you and you see a part of you that wants things to be different, a part of you that has an idea of how things should be different, in what way do you want them to be different? Ask yourself where you learned that it should be different in that way? Who said things should go the way you say they should? Let's have some feedback about your experience. What did you observe as I was inquiring? What did you experience?

Student: I noticed that I was worried that people would reject the new people in the room. I feel real responsible for everybody in here.

A.H. Almaas: Responsible for people here?

S: Yes. Responsible for people's attitudes. I was afraid someone would say something to hurt the new people's feelings. I don't want them to feel rejected.

AH: What else?

S: I was going through the same thing; I was sizing up the new people wondering who I could get to know well.

S: I was doing the same thing, but under that was a desire not to listen to you. I didn't want to listen. I didn't want to admit that I could learn anything by listening to you.

AH: That's true. You can't learn anything by merely listening to me. Very true.

S: I was just feeling good about myself and where I am. In a way I was hoping the new people would feel as uncomfortable as I did the first time I came here, because I know how much I learned from that in the beginning. But they should enjoy themselves too.

S: I found myself being irritated by your talk some-what because it seemed like one of those lowest common denominator talks, and feeling sort of superior. I've been doing this for three years, so I don't have to listen too hard or pay attention now. I noticed I didn't feel like throwing everybody new out of the room the way I did the last time three new people appeared. I was also trying to recognize their type on the enneagram. I was mainly interested that I don't feel threatened by the new people the way I have before. I also feel somehow I have to set an example, and get everything right and act right because they'll be watching me for clues as to how to be.

S: Basically I was feeling good and sort of excited about new people being here, about new faces. I was expecting to feel threatened by the new people coming in and I wasn't at all. That really felt good.

S: I was feeling so threatened about being here—like I wasn't good enough. I wasn't sure how I would fit in. And I thought about how many times in my life I invest strangers with powers that they in fact don't have.

S: I'm feeling resistant to being here. It's a beautiful day. There's a million things I'd rather be doing. I felt very judgmental about feeling that way. I made the choice to be here, so why can't I just experience my choice?

S: I used to see you as a pecan pie and the more people there were the smaller the slice I would get. I don't think I see you that way any more.

S: I feel awkward about being here, very strange. And I'm also feeling how much I need to be perfect, to do everything perfectly, just right.

AH: Now I'll try to point out the common elements in all your comments which are very important for us to understand if we are going to do this work seriously. The most common element, if you notice, is the commentary about what is happening. We do not allow what is happening to just be what is happening, to take its course. The most common thing we do is feel that things should be a certain way. We wish to change things, to have things be a certain way. This attitude prevails in your comments and also in the thoughts and feelings of those of you who didn't make comments. Something in our minds is looking at what is there, saying, "Should it be that way or not?" You look at your feelings and what do you do? Do you just feel your feelings, or are you asking whether you should feel a certain way? Is it good or bad? "I like this, I don't like this." The commentary is always going on about your feelings or about someone else's feelings or presence or actions. Some of the things you spoke about sounded nice. "I want other people to feel comfortable, welcomed. I want to feel good and happy." The comments can go one way or the other, but the general tendency is to want things a particular way. That particular way may change from one person to the other, but each one of us thinks things ideally should be a certain way. "Ideally, I should be here and feel good and feel welcoming toward everybody." Or, "Ideally, I should get as much as I want." Or, "Ideally, I should not be nervous at all." Or, "Ideally, I should not need this work at all. Ideally, I should be somewhere else water-skiing. Ideally, the chair I'm sitting on should be a sofa." Right?

What is implied in these thoughts? Whether you think something positive or negative, isn't it implied that you know how things should be? Isn't it implied that you feel qualified to judge reality? Isn't it implied that you are qualified to say what you and other people should feel and what should happen or should not happen? In Christian theology this function is reserved for God. He's the One who's supposed to know and decide what happens. But you're always trying to take that role. If you look at it really closely, you will see that every minute you're saying that you know better than God! "Things should be this way, not that way. I should feel this way not that way. There shouldn't be clouds today—I don't like clouds—there should be sun." So, there is always a movement of judgment. There is always a desire for things to be different and that desire for things to be different is dependent on your ideas about how things should be different.

These ideas about how things should be different—about how you and other people should feel and experience things, about what is good and what is bad—are what some people call our "ton of cabbage." If you remember the story, "The Islanders," you're told that you can't learn to swim as long as you're carrying your ton of cabbage. What is swimming? To swim is to live, to live freely. I'm not saying this so that you make more commentaries on your experience, and judge it even more. If you do, you're just adding another ton of cabbage. The point is not to judge yourself but to just look at the situation, to see how you always make judgments. Do you see that you are always making a judgment?

It's a simple, logical inference that if you really knew how you should feel, how others should feel, and how things should go, by now you would have achieved everything you wanted in your life and be happy, contented, fulfilled and free.

When people come here to work on themselves, to understand and develop themselves, they usually say they want to be different, they want to change. They want to change their lives and they want to change themselves. However, if you really want to change yourself, if you want yourself and your life to be different, could that change occur according to your already existing conceptions about how things should go? Would that be a change or would that just be a continuation of what has been?

What we find here is that we're trying to change things but we're always trying to change them according to our old ideas about how things should go. But your ideas about how things should go are the product of your present condition. How else could it be? The way you go about wanting things to change will only keep them the same. You can't do anything else.

You're always trying to change yourself, right? "I'm a miserable person. I want to be happy. So this is what I'm going to do about it." Well, your ideas of how things should go are simply the product of how you are now. So how are you going to feel happy if you are acting according to the understanding of someone who is miserable? You can only continue the misery! If you're a jealous person and you say you want to be a loving person so you should do this and this, you're just going to continue being jealous, because your idea of how things should go come from how you think of yourself as a jealous person. Your ideas of how love develops will have rules coming out of jealousy. How can such ideas produce love? How can beliefs brought out of suffering produce happiness? An idea can only perpetuate its own nature. If you're a frightened person, fear will be a thread running through all your ideas. And such ideas can only produce more fear.

It's an interesting dilemma that we find ourselves in. The general tendency of the personality is to try to change things according to our own preconceptions. How else can we do it? We can only act according to what we already know. And we don't know freedom and fulfillment.

Where does that leave us? If you really listen and absorb what I have said, you'll notice some fear, or anxiety. If you begin to understand what I am saying, you will realize that you have to let go of your preconceptions and start fresh. We need to approach this work with an unknowing mind, a mind that is open to what is new, rather than a mind that is like a wheel running according to what is old.

You want to change, which means you want something new. But in your attempt to change, you're continuing the old, because you're trying to change according to the ideas, the plans and the conditions of the old. I'm talking about actual change; I'm not talking about what most people call change. What most people call change is to make a stick a little longer or shorter. But it's all the same stick. That's not change. If you are suffering and you want to be happy, it's not the same thing as making a stick longer. You might be less miserable but you won't be happy. Happiness and misery are two entirely different categories. It's like the difference between a stick and a cloud.

You want to change, because you want to be happy and free. That's human. Everyone wants to be happy. It's natural to want to be happy because happiness is our natural state. When we're not happy, we feel that something is missing and we want to change. However, we need to question how we go about it. I'll use an analogy to examine the situation more closely. Let's say you have a car, a Rabbit. You know nothing about cars. You've never studied about engines. You don't know about cylinders or drive shafts or carburetors. You're driving in the car and there's a little noise. "Terrible! I need to fix it." You open the hood and you go about changing one thing or another. You have no idea what's producing the noise. Even if you knew what's producing it, what's producing it is connected to everything else in the car. How can you change anything? You would mess everything up.

When you're working on yourself, you're like this car you don't know anything about. You don't know anything about yourself. Something goes wrong. First you judge that it's bad and then you try to fix it by doing this or that. You have no idea how this is connected to other things in you. And, as I say, the situation is worse because you're riding in the car and you say it doesn't feel right.

It's clunking; it doesn't go fast enough. Something about it is not right. What should you do about it? Take it to a mechanic to change the spark plugs, put a new engine in it, or buy better gasoline? You have a Rabbit. It doesn't go exactly the way you feel it should. Finally somebody tells you that maybe you should get another kind of car. A BMW. You get the BMW. "Ah, that's more like it. More solid. Smoother." Right? But after a while, it's not exactly right either. You begin to be discontent with the car. Now you could trade in the BMW for something else. But suppose that the issue here is not to change the feeling by doing something about the car. Maybe the feeling you're after will not come from a car. Maybe the feeling you're missing, what you call happiness, will arise only if you are flying in an airplane. So the change that needs to happen is not to change your car to make it better, or to change it from one brand of car to a different one. Maybe you need an airplane.

And perhaps you'll be discontent as long as you tinker around with your car. You're used to driving a Rabbit. What you want is to drive an airplane. But you believe you need to drive a BMW.

So what you need is not a car mechanic, not different parts or a different car. Not even a major overhaul! You need a radical change, a complete shift of perspective. You need to know how to fly in the air rather than drive on the freeway. That's the kind of change that happens in this work. But when you sit there saying, "No, I want it to be like this," you're tinkering with your car, trying to make it fly. You can only make things worse.

Trying to make your car fly is hopeless. It won't work that way. You can only continue doing the same thing, which is driving on the freeway. You can drive faster, slower, more smoothly—but you're not going to fly. Basically, you'll continue doing the same thing.

Wanting things a certain way, wanting things to be different, wanting to change yourself, wanting your situation to change, wanting feelings to change is not an effective approach, because you can only want things to change according to what you know. What needs to happen is something you don't know and the only way it can happen is for you to stop the movement of trying to change things and just let yourself be open and say, "I don't know what's supposed to happen. Why don't I stop all this business and just allow things to happen." If anything new is going to happen, it's got to come from somewhere else, not from your ideas about things.

What we are doing, in effect, is trying to learn how to get used to flying an airplane, when all we are used to is driving a Rabbit. If you understand what I am saying, you'll see that there is no other way. If you continue doing things the same way as you always have, you can only produce the same results.

It is understandable that you want to change. Change is natural. Change is the actual state of reality. Reality is always in flux, in constant change and transformation. Life is change, continual movement and transformation and renewal. When it is allowed to unfold, life is always fresh and new. Creativity is the movement of life. When you allow yourself to be, instead of trying to change, you become a creative person. Life is creativity, unfoldment, transformation, in ways you can't even imagine yet.

Wanting to change has nothing to do with change. Trying to change has nothing to do with the natural movement of change. The natural movement of change is an unfoldment. It's not something you can direct.

The problem here is not that you want change but do not change. The problem is that you are not allowing the change because you want it a certain way. Suppose you have a garden with a big rose bush. The first time you see this bush you decide it should have irises. The moment a bud appears, you cut it off—"That's not an iris! When are the irises going to start blooming? This tree isn't growing right. I've been giving it everything—water, sun, good care—but I don't see any irises!"

It's a rose bush. "I don't care if it's a rose bush. I like irises!" Why do you like irises? "That's what my mother and father grew. What else would I like? That's the only right thing to have. Irises!"

The natural movement may go a certain way, but all you know is something from your experience in the past. But the past is done, and now something really new is happening. You're saying, "No, no! I want something wonderful that happened three years ago when I was in love and it was wonderful and that's the feeling that I want to have happen." Or you want something that happened when you were in your mother's womb, or at your mother's breast, or in your father's lap. You want to bring back an old feeling.

That's stagnation. That's staying the same way. So every time a new bud appears, you chop it off, and complain about how things don't change. You don't look at what's actually unfolding.

Suppose you're thirty-five years old and you're about to turn thirty-six. You have no idea what being thirty-six years old is going to be like. You've never been thirty-six before. And you feel that at thirty-six you should feel exactly as you did when you were thirty-six months old. So you're watching, and the moment you see something slightly different from your expectation, you go to a therapist, thinking something's wrong. This sort of judgment is an attempt to force reality to go a certain way.

You might read many how-to books in order to figure out how to change yourself, but the people who wrote the books are just like you. They only know from their experience. They don't know what's supposed to happen to you. You read about the Buddha, and his life three thousand years ago, and you conclude that you should be like him. But who knows whether a realized human being in our time should be like a Buddha?

You don't know how things should go. If you try to force them to go a certain way, there will be a conflict, stagnation, and the stunting of growth and development. Then you feel miserable because things aren't going the way you think they should go. When you feel unhappy, it's because things are not the way you think they should be. You're making a judgment about reality.

Let's say that you discover that you have a disease and you're going to die in two years. You become frightened and miserable.

Why? Who says it would be better for you to live another thirty years? Maybe if you die in two years many things will happen. How do you know, really? Maybe you'll go to greener pastures. Some people don't like these pastures and want to go to greener pastures so they kill themselves. Again, this is interfering with reality. A really different approach would be to accept things just the way they are.

You believe in your ideas about how things should be, for instance, what constitutes happiness and success. You are always trying to live your life according to these ideas. But this closes you off from that openness that will reveal what's actually unfolding. You are rejecting reality and restricting the possibilities of what could happen.

Now you are asking yourselves, "So what can we do?" But let's look at that question—what is the motivation behind it? Isn't the motivation that you want something, and want to know how to go about getting it? And isn't that wanting determined by your usual beliefs and ideas? Aren't you then engaged again in the same movement, continuing the same old reality? The alternative to this pattern will appear only if we completely understand what we are discussing.

To seek an alternative is already a judgment that things need to be different. This judgment is based on certain basic beliefs—that you should be happy in your life, that you should live as long as possible, that it is better to be beautiful than not beautiful, better to be rich than poor, better to be a success than a failure. Every day you put the same patterns, same ideas, and same hopes in front of you. They may be modified here and there, but they are basically the same. We carry our past with us. If you look at your life, there is no present, no future; your mind is always in the past.

You are furnishing your future, all the time, by continuing your past. Everyone wants to continue in the same way, yet you wonder why your life does not seem fresh or new, why instead, it feels like a swamp. You say you want newness, life, freshness, change, transformation. But this would mean that the past is left in the past. Is it possible for us to be here without the past?

What I'm saying is not original. Every spiritual teacher says the same thing: the point is not success or happiness, the point is to be real. I'm saying this now so that you can understand the situation, not so that you do something about it.

We are trying to understand what it is to live life, not the way our parents said it should be, or the way the books say it should be, not according to our ideas or other people's ideas, but the way it is—how things are according to reality. We want to learn how to let the rose bush produce roses, how to let it be a rose bush rather than trying to change it into something else.

We haven't yet explored the extent to which we try to control things, how much we try to twist reality's arm.

We need to see the situation as completely and as accurately as possible.

The problem is not that we want to be happy, but that we are going about it in the wrong way. When we really see that we are going about it in the wrong way, we quit. And then life can unfold on its own. We cannot make it unfold. We can quit our rejection, our judgment, our intolerance, but we will quit these patterns only when we completely and totally see what they are doing—that they are hurting us.

We still don't understand that our attitudes, ideas, and beliefs are actually responsible for our suffering. We pay lip service to this idea but we don't know it completely and totally. So we continue in our old patterns. The work we do here is simply to see the picture completely, seeing exactly what it is you are doing and how that affects reality.

This is the way that real freedom, actual change, will come about. To live in freedom and absolute fulfillment, we need a complete, radical shift, and such a shift can occur only when there is a complete understanding of what we are actually doing. All the work you do here is based on understanding what you do and how you interfere with the natural process. If you try to do anything other than understand the situation, your effort will be a blockage, a resistance, an interference. You cannot make yourself grow; you can only cease to interfere. You cannot make yourself happy; you can only stop your judgments. Growth and expansion are natural; they are the life force itself. And you cannot predict its direction.

If you recall the times when you have experienced a release, when there was an opening, you will see it was always by your understanding something, by your somehow getting out of the way, by your letting go of some belief, some resistance, some idea. This never happens by your accomplishing something. It happens always through losing something. We should write on the door to this room, "Whenever you feel you are going to lose something, celebrate!" Because you can only lose what is false. What is real cannot be lost. What is real is you—that can't be lost. What can be lost is the false. So whenever you feel you are going to lose something, welcome the feeling.

You can only lose your ideas, your assumptions, your blindness, your blockages, your misunderstanding, your prejudice. Everything we do here is oriented toward seeing exactly what is happening right now. We never try to make things happen. We always look at what is here, what you are doing, what's causing you to do it. When a student comes to a new understanding, that is when there is an openness, a release, an expansion, a change.

When it is allowed, change can only be good, can only be expansion. The natural movement is toward greater abundance. If you are not experiencing expansion and abundance, it's because you are interfering. There is no other reason. There is no devil tempting you, no one conspiring against you. It is not because of the economy or the Republicans. It is you getting in your own way, always. You are the one interfering. It's true the state of the economy may mean you earn less money, but that's not what is making you miserable or scared.

Suppose it is true that you don't have a job and you don't have money. Why be scared? What does that do for you? "Well," you say, "I don't have a job so I might starve to death, so I'm scared." Does getting scared make you live longer? You can go scream and have a temper tantrum, but that will not prolong your life. Ultimately, our misery and our fear is all our doing. It is an interference with our own natural process.

This insight is quite promising. If your attitude is ultimately up to you, freedom is possible. If your life were in someone else's hands or in the hands of the devil, you wouldn't have a chance!

Our orientation here is always toward truth. It is about allowing, understanding and accepting what is there. This doesn't mean that you need to feel resignation. It means accepting and being open to what is there and what happens. That is not resignation. You are completely allowing your experience without saying no to it, without saying yes to it. If you are really open in this way, things will change on their own. Nothing will stay the same.

I am not interested in changing people. I am not here to change you or to make you feel better or happier. This does not mean I am against change, nor that there be no change. We do not focus on the change itself, because you can focus on change only from your old perspective. The best way to go about this work is to explore the truth. If there is going to be change, the change will come from the truth itself. I cannot determine it; you cannot determine it. The truth itself, reality, will determine it.

I don't try to change anyone; I don't know how you should be. Who am I to say you should be this way, or that way, with this kind of job, or that kind of life? I can only look at the situation and help you understand it, and from that something will unfold.

The only thing you can do is to be as aware as possible. Be conscious of yourself, your situation, your reactions. Consciousness, awareness and attention, make it possible to understand what is happening. It is also possible to see the truth, to see how you are interfering and to understand how your interference is producing your conflict and suffering. When you see this completely, you will stop interfering.

When you do stop, the truth will emerge. What is real in you, your essence, will help you only when you cease to interfere. What is real and true in us, what is alive, what is loving, what is genuine, will emerge and assist us only when we take the attitude of being aware and paying attention without trying to change anything. If your attitude is judgment and rejection, that in itself is a resistance to our true nature. When you are resisting it, of course it cannot assist you. You have to meet it half way, without resistance. Then it will emerge and dissolve the misery which resistance and blockage produce. The misery will melt away.

The real cannot be expected, cannot be planned for. It will be a continual surprise. If you work for something and you get it, that something is something you already know. It's already old. Real life is an endless manifestation and unfoldment of surprises. I am surprised a lot by the things I see. Life is full of surprises when you really don't know how things are going to be. We need to allow ourselves to be surprised by our experience and by ourselves.

Unfoldment involves continual change and transformation. If you try to hold on to something, even happiness or love, and keep it a certain way, it will stagnate and become sour or bitter. This is not an easy lesson to learn, but it is possible to learn it.

In my own process, I had no idea what was supposed to happen. I had my assumptions, beliefs, and what I heard from people, or read. Something would develop that was good and wonderful and I would think, "This must be it." The next thing I knew I'd be hit on the head and something else was happening. I thought *that* was it. This went on for years. Every time something new happened, I thought, "This must be it." I finally got clobbered enough times to forget about trying to keep things a certain way.

Finally, I learned that there is no end. The end is only an attitude about an end. In terms of experience of life, there is continual surprise. Each surprise is bigger and more completely unexpected than the one before. The life of essence, the true life, has nothing to do with expectations and plans and beliefs.

You might believe that you are a body and you are driving a Rabbit. You might find that that is not true; you are really a star and you are driving a spaceship. We try to feel secure by being continually the same. And that need for security is part of the reason we continue doing what we always do. Even though we might be miserable, and complain about it, we continue to do it because there is some security there. It is our way of continuing our familiar ego identity.

If something completely different happened, you'd say, "Wait a minute, that's scary, I don't know what happened to me. I know myself to be somebody who drives a Rabbit and suddenly I'm a star driving a spaceship? That's not me. That's not what my father and mother said I could do, not what my birth certificate says. What's going to happen? I think I'm losing it!" Yes, you're losing it. You're losing your Rabbit and your old ideas about who you are and about what's supposed to happen! True freedom is allowing things to happen the way they naturally happen. If you interfere, that interference itself is the suffering, is actually the core of the suffering.

When Buddha spent the last night under the Bodhi tree, he said, "I am going to stay here until I do it. I am not going to get up until I achieve enlightenment." So he started with his intense determination, and his desire and ideas of what it would be like. He sat there without moving until dawn and he came to the understanding that his determination to change was the problem. This is my perspective of the Buddha's story for our discussion today. It's a paradox, but what else can you do about it?

It's true, wanting any change is by itself the resistance, but we have acknowledged the situation, and seen that at the present you cannot do it any other way. We have to accept this situation and live with it.

The truth is your nature. If there were no possibility of knowing truth then none of this would be of any value. The question is whether you can do this work without effort, and just let what is there be there, and explore it. That doesn't require effort. Effort is needed in resisting, not in seeing the truth. Seeing the truth is the relinquishing of effort. This is the true manifestation of will. We all think that will means effort. Will, we think, involves using force to go somewhere or to accomplish something. But that is not the correct understanding of will.

Will involves surrender to the truth, which is the effortless being of what is. Will is actually effortless, complete spontaneity, complete letting go. It is surrender. People think that to surrender is to let go of your will. This is not true. To surrender is to have your will completely, objectively.

S: Everyone here has done something else in a search to make them feel better, to make them feel complete. You say that when we see the truth we know it, we feel it and sense it, but all those sensibilities you're talking about are so deeply conditioned by someone else, that every time you think you've seen the truth about something, ten years later you realize that wasn't the truth at all, it was given to you by somebody else.

AH: What you are saying is an expression of a feeling of hopelessness, and that needs to be looked at and understood.

S: But isn't hopelessness a typical part of the human condition?

AH: It is a typical part of the human condition. But it can be looked at and understood like anything else. Hopelessness makes things stay a certain way, which is blocking the truth. Your hopelessness is not true hopelessness, because it has hope in it. True hopeless-ness does not have hope. Hope means you want things to be a certain way.

S: So my hope is that I hope I will understand what is going on in my life?

AH: Yes, but why do you need to hope? Why not just look and understand? Hope means you are rejecting the situation here, and that you hope for something else. Your hopelessness is not complete. If you are really hope-less you will stop interfering.

S: The real changes I've seen in my life all happened when I was totally beside myself, and feeling that if I didn't stop something, whatever it was, that I would be dead in a few days or minutes. I was feeling desperate, and I don't think people can trust those states.

AH: My dear friend, it is always desperate like that—we just don't see it. You think of physical death as a bad thing. What happens to most people is worse. It's always a desperate condition. This is one of the truths you need to see. You have to look at your assumptions and ideas and see that things could be different from what you think. You thought at one time you were in a desperate situation, and I see that you are always in a des-perate situation. You might cover it over. People cover up their desperateness and hopelessness and everything else. Most of the time people are desperately trying to do something. There is always this feverish movement going on inside, always. If you really look at yourself deeply you will see that.

S: Once you get to the point of understanding these things, then you have to deal with the emotional part, which is the part that doesn't seem to let go. For instance, I understand that my wife may fall in love with another man, but if that actually happened, it would be very difficult, even though I understand it.

AH: It is not true that you have an understanding about it. You think you have understanding about it. If you really have understanding about it, you won't respond that way. You have misunderstanding about it. You read something some place, or someone told you something—that's not understanding. Understanding is when you are feeling it in every cell of your body.

Then change can happen. Not just, "That's understandable—my wife may find somebody else some day. That's the way things are." That's not understanding. That's an idea. Understanding is something much more radical than that. By its very nature it is transformative. When you have an understanding that doesn't transform you, it is not understanding; it is something else.

You see how I am shifting things around. You call something will and it turns out not to be will. You call something understanding and it turns out not to be understanding. You call something hopelessness, and it turns out not to be hopelessness. That's what you find out in time, that everything is really upside down.

We need continually to examine our ideas about things. Your concern is not trivial. I know there is a lot of deep feeling, suffering, and frustration, and I am not taking what you say lightly. But things must be seen the way they are, regardless of how you feel. It's true that people suffer a lot. It is also true that people do not have to suffer so much, and can be fulfilled. I know it is possible. Everyone knows it is possible; but we must go about it without motivation and judgments. We must see the truth itself.

It's not as if you will have a wonderful experience one day and it will change you. "Ah, my kundalini is coming up and now I'm enlightened." Your kundalini can come up and if you don't understand the situation, it will turn to muck. That's what happens to most people.

Ultimately, you will have to give up all techniques and manipulations in order to see what you are really doing.

You don't need to believe me. Take what I'm saying as a proposition and check it for yourself. If you just accept what I say and believe in it, that's not understanding. That's a belief. Right now it is an idea; you have to connect the idea with your experience. To understand it is the freedom. It's a matter of seeing the truth. There is this chance because we have awareness. If we didn't have this awareness, no understanding or freedom could happen. But we do have awareness. The problem people have all the time is that they are restricting that awareness, instead of letting it unfold naturally.

You think you must use effort to make yourself aware. That's not true. Effort always restricts your awareness and you need to see how you are restricting it. It is natural and effortless to be completely aware, but you interfere. It is our nature to be aware. That is why it's possible for you to see the truth. The truth is our nature. Ultimately we are awareness.

What I am saying here is something radically different from what most people think should be happening for them to be happy. What is required is radical. A little modification will not do. In time everything will be upside down. When you start seeing reality, everything will be upside down. Everything. The actual reality is the love, is the fulfillment. It is nothing to be afraid of.

You cannot really understand what we are talking about and also have a question about what to do, about why things are not going right. If you have such questions then you are not understanding what I am saying. You still have judgments and ideas about how things should go. To understand the situation means to be completely open right now to the truth of the situation.

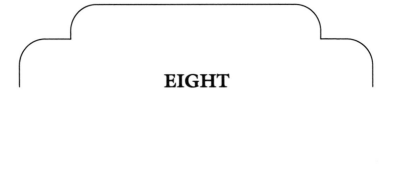

EIGHT

Will

Today we will clarify a certain misunderstanding that almost everyone has. It goes to the root of the way we think. It's a misunderstanding of a certain part of ourselves, and we will see that our usual understanding of this part of ourselves is exactly opposite to the truth. We will explore the quality of will.

As we have seen, when you are trying to make something happen, you are not trusting the natural order; you don't trust that essence itself will manifest in the way it is needed. The first point of departure from this trust is always a rejection of the now. To apply the perspective of basic trust, of true will, you must have the complete confidence that staying completely with what you are experiencing in this moment, will result in what needs to happen, without your having to think about a certain outcome. When the confidence is there, your awareness of exactly what is happening in you will allow you to see that your organism will do the best it can in the situation. Your mind, however, doesn't allow that complete presence in the now; it thinks it knows what is best for you, but of course it knows only what has happened in the past, and can lead you only in ways conditioned by your history. Because you don't know that you have an innate intelligence that knows what needs to be done, you don't allow it to operate. You are always trying to direct it this or that way; and this is what we usually call "will." But when we are directing and controlling ourselves, we are stopping our spontaneity. We are not able to trust, and thus are blocking our true will.

True will is actually nothing but complete surrender to what is experienced in this moment. From the perspective of the adult, true will is complete surrender of what is usually called "will," and so is functionally the opposite. True will does not involve surrender to another person, but to yourself, to life, to your experience, to the truth of now. Surrender to the truth of now does not mean that you see what is happening and don't care. That's not surrender. Surrender means complete willingness to be with your experience, including your emotional reactions, whether they are pleasurable or frustrated. You are steadfast with the truth.

Another way to see true will is to understand that it is simply the attunement to what is natural. What's happening right now is what is natural for us. To say "no" to what is naturally happening is to create a separate, false will that has its own idea about how things are supposed to happen. And as we have seen this can only lead to division and conflict.

The moment we say "no" to our experience, we are using false will. True will is simply letting go of the false will that wants to take our experience somewhere else.

So when we are willing to be completely in the moment, we have a better chance of seeing what is actually there, what is actually happening. If we are saying, "No, I don't want this, I want it to be different," that blocks the experience and gives us less chance of seeing the truth clearly. So when true will is operating, it enhances our awareness of what is there. It allows us to have a more complete and full perception. Only when we have this complete perception can we truly understand what is there. This understanding of what is happening is in itself a discharge, a regulation. When such insight happens it is like an orgasm—it is a release of tension. Just as your mother released your tension when you were hungry or in pain as an infant, allowing a relaxation, the process of simply seeing what is there and understanding it releases what is false in us. Discontent, pain and conflict are not part of our natural state. When you see and release what is false, it goes away. This is the discharge, the regulation. And what remains is what is real.

But usually we are busy trying not to see things as they actually are, so we are always stopping our organism from freely operating the way it naturally operates. When you are discontent, what do you usually do? You say, "I'm dissatisfied because my boyfriend doesn't have sex with me enough these days." And what do you do about it? You try to do something to make him sleep with you more often. If that doesn't work, you might look for someone else. Maybe you have an idea that you're supposed to have these wonderful orgasms, and that's what a boyfriend is for, to give them to you. The boyfriend is nothing but a live dildo. If he doesn't make you feel good on a regular basis, what good is he? That's how we think, because that's how our mothers functioned for us. When you're having a hard time, she's supposed to make you feel better. If not, she's a bad mommy, and you would like to have someone else who would be a good mommy.

But what if we simply stay with the discontent, feel it fully, instead of doing something about it? Just stay with it because it's the truth. This is the true will, in contrast to trying to manipulate the situation with false will.

When we surrender to what we are experiencing in the moment, the will of the essence is free, and will function in the way it is meant to function. If you completely feel your discontent, you will know what it is actually about. It might be because your boyfriend hasn't slept with you. It might be some other reason. If you really stay with the discontent, you might feel it as a lack of satisfaction. You might feel there is no satisfaction in you. Staying with that might reveal the discontent as a kind of hole, as something missing. You might see, "Oh, it's satisfaction that I'm missing." And if you really stay with that you might understand why you have no satisfaction just by being what you are in the moment. Who says you can have satisfaction only after an orgasm? That's what your mind says. But your organism can give you satisfaction at any time, before an orgasm or after it, or regardless of it. If you really stay with that sense of dissatisfaction, you will note that a part of you is absent; and if you stay completely and fully with that absence, and understand it, there will be a release, a discharge. The release will be the return of satisfaction. Then you will see that satisfaction is part of you. It is not the result of an action or a process. It is part of you just as love, joy and compassion are a part of you.

When we try to fill the holes by exerting our will, or what we call our will, we don't allow the natural process of release to happen. When we can stay steadfast with the truth, and align the will with the truth itself, we see in time that the organism will provide what is needed. When there is a need for satisfaction, there is satisfaction. When there is a need for fulfillment, there is fulfillment. When you have real satisfaction, fulfillment and love, you discover many things you thought you needed in your life you don't really need—you wanted them in order to get the fulfillment and satisfaction. When you are not needing to fill holes, your life will be an expression of your satisfaction.

This is a true life, then: instead of trying to get satisfaction, fulfillment, happiness, love, we allow ourselves to have basic trust. Then all that we do, our relationships and all our activities, are an expression of the satisfaction, fulfillment and love. The true life is a spontaneous activity that arises out of our essence, and there is no need for the efforting kind of will. You've got everything. You simply need to see the truth, and what needs to happen just happens. You don't need to do anything about it. The functioning of true will causes you to do what is needed: if you need to go buy something from the store, or to talk with someone about something, the impulse will come spontaneously. You don't need to ruminate about it. All of you have had such experiences, when everything flows spontaneously. You just do what's right. As adult human beings, we actually have the capacity always to do what is right, for ourselves and for everyone else.

We have lost that confidence, that basic trust. And we see that the way to have it is actually to start doing it. It's not something you gain; you actually practice it. You practice it by staying with what is there, by not going along with the usual tendency to reject what is there and try to get something else.

Most of our discontent, pain and discomfort is the result of losing a part of ourselves. It's not because of the economy; it's not because we are ugly or fat or this or that. These are not the real reasons. So trying to get fulfillment by solving these supposed problems doesn't work. The dissatisfaction comes from not allowing ourselves to experience a part of us. We are full of holes, and the only way we can be fulfilled and complete is to stay with those holes so that part of us is allowed to manifest and function. This cannot happen as long as we try to fill our holes with something else.

We are beings who exist or were created a certain way; when we allow ourselves to be the way we are, then everything goes well. That's what we will learn in time, and it may take time: our lack of trust is habitual. We keep believing in the wrong perspective, in our deficiency. But in time we might see that there is no need to believe in it. We are full. We can be complete; that is our natural state. If we allow ourselves to be, naturally, everything will circulate and will happen as it is meant to happen.

One way true will manifests is as a sense of confidence that you can stay with your experience; deeper still is an implicit confidence, which is not from the mind, that staying with what is there is the right thing. It's a trust in oneself—as simple as that. There is no need to hope for anything, no need to desire anything. There is nothing somewhere else to hope for, to desire. Everything is right here, with us; we just need to let it be. And if we don't understand this perspective, we need to explore why, why we are not allowing our organism to function.

We are seeing that our exploration of will has led us back to the perspective of truth. The truth will set you free. Will means staying with the truth. Will functions in the service of truth. And for truth to manifest you don't need effort. Truth is what is there. You need only stop the effort of avoiding seeing what is there. You are always exerting effort, using your will to push something away, to make things different. This is how you stop your will.

This understanding is why many spiritual disciplines state that you must surrender your will. It is true that you must surrender what most people think of as will. But what is usually not seen is that true will exists, and that it is the same thing that most people call surrender. But it's not a sense of surrender to someone or something else. You are surrendering to the truth. What other choice do you have? However painful or pleasurable the experience happens to be, if you stay with it you might discover a deeper truth in it. Actually, when you look fully, squarely at the situation, you see that you have no alternative, except running away. You either experience what is so, or you try to avoid it. And trying to avoid it can only lead to suffering. You cannot change how you feel in the moment. Trying to change what you feel in the moment is like looking at a tree which has green leaves, and saying, "No, I like yellow leaves, I want it to have yellow leaves." But it's not the season for yellow leaves, and you can't change that. You could paint the tree and cover up the green leaves; this covering up is what we do all the time with our feelings. But we can't really change the nature of things.

If we learn the lesson that the way it is, is the way it should be, if we accept that, then everything will run smoothly, and in fact will function perfectly in many more ways than you expect—in what will seem like magical, miraculous ways.

Of course, having full confidence and trust in life, and knowing that things happen spontaneously, does not mean that you don't act in your life. I don't mean that there is no activity, no action, no preferences in your life. When true will is functioning, activities and preferences come from a real place. They are spontaneous expressions of who you are, not reactions to something you don't like. They are expressions of the truth of the situation, rather than attempts to change that truth.

This perspective on will might be difficult to accept, even to see as possible. It is difficult because of our habitual thought. But it is actually the situation, and maybe in time you will come to see it. As you learn this perspective you will live more in the natural state which is positive, loving, sweet and blissful. Only our misunderstandings, which lead to contractions, blockage and a cycle of suffering, keep us from this natural state.

The usual use of will is actually a contraction in the body. It is a hard place in us, which we use as a stepping stone for action. When people say they have their will, they are referring to a certain hardness in the body, from which they feel they can act; they can spring out and feel supported in their action; or they feel they have something under their feet, and that they won't fall. But if you look closely at that hardness, that stepping stone, you can identify it as a tension in the body. You might feel that you can't live your life without that tension; you have learned to contract certain parts of you, near your heart, to make a little hardness, and from that little hardness you feel you can act. You feel if the hardness is not there, you will be completely empty, and will just fall, unable to do anything. But what the contraction actually does, ultimately, is close your heart. It closes the love, the joy, and the satisfaction. Using false will always goes against the heart.

Letting go of the false will might be scary; you might feel as if you are falling into emptiness; you might wonder whether you will be able to function without it. But when real will is present there is no feeling of fear, no feeling that the emptiness is bad and that you will fall into it. If there is no true will, and no false will, the experience is fear. Basically it is a fear of falling, of no support, of no recourse. But when there is emptiness, which is the lack of a contraction, and the presence of true will, you experience openness rather than fear.

This situation leaves us in a dilemma. We are afraid to let go of our false will, our hardness and rigidity, because we are afraid we are going to fall on our faces, with no support and nothing to hold on to. We will have nothing to push against in order to act. It will just be a huge vacuity. To avoid this feeling we harden ourselves, create a false will so that there will be something under us from which we can spring into action. This happens because you believe you need something to support you, and the belief creates a blockage against the true will. It is the belief itself that creates the blockage, which appears near the solar plexus. When you see this belief, the blockage goes away, and you see that emptiness, rather than something you might fall into, is an openness from which spontaneous action arises. Then instead of fear there is confidence.

So we see that will and fear are connected. The loss of basic confidence makes us block our will, which then creates a fear that without the false will we will have no support. We feel we will be vulnerable and defenseless, unsupported, groundless, with nothing under our feet. We feel our needs will just collapse under us if we let go of the false will. This might actually happen momentarily, until the true will is felt. With the true will, you do not feel as if you are being supported, you simply feel the absence of the fear and of the need for support. It feels like an openness, and emptiness, a big space in which to experience life. You feel that all kinds of possibilities are there, and no intentional action is needed. Things will just emerge out of that openness, spontaneously.

When things are happening spontaneously, there is no need for struggle. So there is no need, for instance, when you are investigating something about yourself, to keep squinting at yourself with your brow tight. Just be there and be aware. The insight will emerge by itself. There is confidence that things will just work out. Whatever perception is needed will arise like a flowering. It's a natural process, and it will happen. This openness, this freedom, is both the end result of allowing our natural functioning, our true will, and the method itself, the way to go about our work.

When we don't need that hardness as a stepping stone, the emptiness will be an openness in the heart, for the fulfillment, the love, the joy, satisfaction and content-ment—all the things we seek in our lives. It will simply manifest and flow like a fountain. But we are closing the fountain by creating the hardness that we think is what we need to accomplish our fulfillment. Then we ask "Why doesn't it work? I've done this and this, and still I'm not content." Well you are actually working to block it, all the time.

Ultimately, true will manifests as an understanding. It's not as if something is there that will do something for you. It's an understanding that the organism, the life force, knows what needs to be done in the best, most efficient way. It's a confidence in yourself. If the true will is operating you experience it as confidence and trust. There's a complete harmony. Then you are not dividing yourself with a part of you saying, "This is no good, let me change it." You aren't always looking for your boyfriend to give you an orgasm. It might happen or not; if so, it will be an expression of love, of fullness. It will not arise out of a need. But until we experience this we will feel that we need the boyfriend to give us orgasms, or whatever else we think we need to feel loved and comforted.

Complete freedom comes from seeing the futility of effort and hope, by giving up attaining anything, and just being there. You come here and think you are going to accomplish all kinds of things, and you are told to give up your hope. Desire and hope are an attempt to have the will which blocks the true will.

So true will is like the grounding, the implicit grounding that serves as a confidence that things will flow. It's hard to describe exactly, because I'm talking about it as if it is something you think in your mind. It isn't; that's why I use the word "implicit." It means you function from an innate feeling and understanding that things flow. True will is right in this moment; it's a complete openness to what's happening right now. You might understand it in your mind, but in time your understanding needs to become implicit. You don't need to think about it, you just live your life.

There is a certain practice we do for understanding and freeing the will: what we call taking aims. This practice is paradoxical, because it seems to be the manifestation of the false will. That is how it can seem at the beginning. But we are trying to use our will to stay steadfast with the truth when we take aims. The aim is not to accomplish something: it is to be in the present, to see the truth, always. If you want to understand a certain issue, you take an aim to do some action relative to that issue, so that you will be able to understand it. For instance, you might want to understand your desire to get recognition from other people. So you take an aim that for the next month you will observe how you try to get recognition from others. Or for the next week, for a half hour every day, you will not do anything to get recognition from people. That is taking an aim. In time this will lead to the perception of the true operation of the will. However, you will for some time confuse this with the false will; that's fine, it will create a question to deal with. Working with aims is one way to stay steadfast with the truth on your own, in your own space, so that you will be less dependent on the group. Taking an aim always involves stating exactly what you will do, and how often. The precision is an important part of it.

Student: That hardness you spoke of—for me it's like strapping on a penis to go out into the business world, and I notice it creates problems when I come back into my home; it's like we have a battle of penises. I find it difficult to drop that around my husband. We're just realizing that we've always done this.

A.H. Almaas: That's a defensive kind of will. The penis means a hardness, an aggressiveness, which we believe will is. We think it is something aggressive and active, while true will is receptive. Your false will is an attempt to defend yourself, and you need to understand why you do it that way. One of the symbols for the true will is a crescent moon, which is receptive. The crescent moon with the star in the center represents the receptivity to oneself, to your true self. So the receptivity is to the truth of oneself.

You can be active, but you don't have to be active in a defensive and hard way. If you feel you must do that, you have a misunderstanding, as we talked about it today. You can investigate with this perspective, staying with it when you are feeling that way, rather than trying to change it. Trying to change it would involve using the same hardness, trying to use the penis against itself. Instead, ask yourself, "What is the penis all about, what makes me need to use an imaginary penis?"

In this culture we usually think of will as masculine, a hard masculinity. But ultimately, the will is feminine. The true relationship of the will to essence is a receptivity to the truth, an attunement with reality.

S: From a practical standpoint, the whole business culture is built on the basis of goals, planning, projecting of the false will. How can you function the natural way when the society is the opposite?

AH: It's true that the whole society is based on this false perspective. But you can accept the culture and see how the natural, true part of you will behave in this situation. It can be done; business can be done from this perspective. The way we usually think is, "This is where things are supposed to go, and how do we get from here to there?" The natural perspective, however, is like a river running down. It will go the easiest way, with the intelligence moving it step by step. That is how essence functions. It will go exactly the way it needs to go, and that will be the easiest way possible. When we don't have trust that things will naturally flow, we try to push the river one way or another. What we end up doing is making things much more difficult. There is an in-between stage of understanding which we need to investigate: "What am I doing here? Why am I pushing the river? Why do I need to do that? If I allow the natural thing to happen, how will it go?"

Society does go against the flow, because it is based on personality, not on essence. So when you are doing the right thing, you will feel that everything will go wrong and everyone will disagree with you. It's true, few people will agree with you, and then it's very hard to continue to trust yourself. The pressure from the outside is immense. So you need to increasingly stay with your own truth.

S: Is the frustration in the environment which blocks the will when you are a child, the same as negative merging?

AH: Yes. Negative merging is undischarged frustration. And because the frustration isn't discharged we lose or fail to develop confidence. But this undischarged frustration is nothing but an undischarged blockage on the physical level which reflects the loss of confidence on the mental level.

S: It seems to me that because of our pattern of avoiding the truth, avoiding the present, it takes an effort to stay with the truth.

AH: If you really look at yourself, you will see that you are not staying in the present because you are exerting an effort not to stay in the present. The natural thing is to be in the present. If you are not staying in the present, you are exerting some effort, probably unconscious, not to see what is there. So at first going against that tendency to reject the present truth does require an effort. We have seen that the steadfast openness to the truth and to what naturally arises out of the truth is what will in time allow the true will to function.

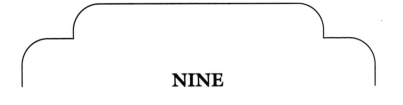

NINE

Self and Selflessness

Today's talk is part of a series in which we're looking at a certain way of seeing and understanding things.

Today we will talk about self and selflessness and further elucidate this perspective. It is not easy to see or to understand, and even when it is seen and understood, it is not easy to accept or follow. If this point of view is not understood, accepted and integrated, then you will continue living your life from the ordinary point of view that you have always had. This means you'll continue to live the same kind of life, and any changes will just be variations on a theme. This point of view will take a few years to understand or accept.

Our usual perspective is the self perspective or ego point of view. It is the view you live according to and adhere to most closely. You believe in this point of view so much that you are willing to sacrifice your life for it. What is this self perspective, this ego point of view?

You, and everyone you know, believes that you have a self and that self has needs, desires, hopes, plans, rights, preferences. You also believe that self needs to be supported, protected, satisfied and gratified. You believe you must get things for that self, and that the dreams and the plans for that self are what life is all about—to satisfy those dreams and ideas, plans and desires. That is basic for everybody. Your particular dream or plan might be different from that of somebody else, but the dreams or plans or endeavors are always related to yourself. Everything is for that self, to support that self, to enhance that self, to expand that self. Everybody has his own territory of self, like islands separate from everyone else's islands. You're always trying to protect that island so nobody else can take it over. You defend it and you beautify it as much as possible in order make it the best island around. You have all kinds of ideas and schemes about how that island should be, and you are very clear that your island is not anybody else's island.

There are as many islands as there are people in the world, and you believe that your self, your island is separate and distinct, not just from other islands, but from the rest of the universe. If you examine what you do, won't you see that you are continually involved in this island, modifying it, rearranging it, reorganizing it?

How aware are you of other islands? Not very. Your awareness of other islands is colored, even determined, by your concerns about how to protect and enhance your island. There is no true interest in the other islands for themselves. When you think of another island, it's how to get something from it, or how those other islands are blocking your view.

The reference point is always the self. Every feeling, thought, every action, every decision, every plan, every complaint is related to that self. This point of view is so common that most people don't think about it—what else could it be? That's how life is. Life is all these islands trying to be the best or the worst, depending on what plans you have for that island.

Sometimes there are wars between the islands. Sometimes there are friendships. But both wars and friendships happen from the perspective of the island, with reference to you—what you'll get from it and what you won't get, what you like or dislike about it, how it makes you feel and your opinions about it.

There are all kinds of islands. Some are very rich, very big, very prosperous, very happy. Some are small, poor, dilapidated. Some islands carry through on great plans—have fine buildings, big advancements, great development. Other islands have a hard time, suffer and don't have much to show. Some islands work to destroy themselves. But regardless of what state the island is in— prosperous, or suffering, or working on growth and development—it's still an island and this is your point of view. This is your blueprint, and as far as you're concerned that's what life is all about.

So whether it is pain or pleasure, happiness or suffering, it is happening to a particular island. The common theme is that all the experiences occur within that perspective of self, of the ego.

Reflect for a minute on what really happens in your process. You may be working on yourself, becoming more aware of yourself, and even trying to help other people. But all the time you are an island. Your mind is full of monologues, dialogues, ideas, feelings, reactions, plans, memories, accusations, all kinds of things. It's turmoil, a storm which has nothing to do with anything outside.

How often do you ever think of someone else, really think of someone else just for who they are?

When we think of people, we are concerned with either liking them or not liking them. We're angry with them or we love them. There's something we don't want from them or there's something we do want from them. We push them away or draw them towards us. Whatever we do, it has to do with ourselves. Very rarely do we actually look at the other person, or any object for that matter, without relating it first and primarily to ourselves.

This is a description, not a judgment. This is the state of affairs. Even when we act in humanitarian ways, serving or helping people, isn't there some turmoil and anxiety over whether or not you're doing it right, being loving enough, helpful enough? This is the same ego perspective. You are not as concerned with other people as you are with yourself. You are thinking primarily of yourself in the name of love and service.

When you want to please people, why do you want to please them? When you do something for somebody, why do you want to do this? You want to please them from your own point of view, for your own reasons. Then you get disappointed if they are not appreciative. You feel your love or your gifts are not accepted. Regardless of what situation you are in and what you feel, you're like a shell full of reactions that bounce around inside you like ping-pong balls. "Am I comfortable? Did I do the right thing? Will they like me? Did I make the best choice? Does that person really understand what I said?" All this is going on inside the shell. Ping-pong, ping-pong, ping-pong! From the outside this looks pretty weird. Most of the time what's happening outside has nothing to do with what's going on inside, all the ping-pong balls bouncing back and forth. Whether you're feeling happy or miserable, it's the same basic point of view, the same basic perspective.

There's an island with boundaries. "Whatever is inside these boundaries is mine. What happens is mine, me, for me." This is the "I" perspective, the self perspective, the ego point of view. It's not that this point of view is a part of you, it is you.

Look at a mountain. It goes up, there's snow on the top. Do you ever just look at a mountain? Or do you look at it through the lens of this self perspective? Do you just look at the mountain, or are you feeling this or that about it? Are you thinking it reminds you of this, it's associated with that? Maybe you want to go skiing or mountain climbing. Maybe it makes you feel small or big. You see the mountain only as it relates to you, not the mountain as a mountain on its own.

So you never really see a mountain. Never! What you see is yourself reflected in the mountain. What you see is your own island with a mirror outside. The same thing happens with every object and person you encounter. This is how you function, how you have always functioned, how you feel you're always going to function, how everyone else functions.

What does this mean? The first implication is that you don't see things or people for themselves. You don't see them objectively. There's no objective perception or experience of anything. You don't really see a mountain. You don't really know a person. To really know people means to look at them without any point of view of your own. You cannot then look at them from your perspective of your ideas, your standards, your lens.

Another implication is that you don't see what is really there. You have no idea of what a mountain is. The only way it is possible for you to see the mountain is to not have your point of view and let yourself be the mountain. Instead, you let the mountain be like you, and you form an opinion about it, an idea which has to do with your past experience, not with the mountain in front of you.

Another implication is that you have a barrier, a veil between you and what is there, between you and reality. When you hear this, it might not sound so serious. "Okay, so I don't see reality as it is."

Right now, you may be looking at yourself in a critical or judgmental way. If you are doing this, aren't you looking at yourself from the same perspective?

We're trying to be aware of the situation, to understand it. We are not trying to change it. If you change it you can only change it according to the blueprint you already have—you would only have a variation on the usual theme.

Another implication of this ego point of view is that there is a restriction, a boundedness to your experience. You are walled in. You are in jail! You might entertain yourself with all kinds of things in that jail, but you're still in a jail. You can't leave the island. You don't want to leave it. You can't imagine leaving it! You believe that leaving the island means that you will drown. So you're always going over the same terrain in different ways—sometimes on a bicycle, sometimes in a car, sometimes in a balloon. But it's always the same terrain.

Another aspect of this point of view is its separateness from other islands. If you have your own island, don't you need to be on guard, alert? Don't you need to protect it from threat? You are always afraid something may happen to it, so you need a strong army, and you put a lot of your energy and resources into defense. When you're not trying to defend your island, you're busy trying to get things for your island. Your life is a variation on two themes: protection and acquisition. You want more approval, more success, more money, more recognition, more knowledge, more experience, more pleasure. You make your island stronger, more enduring, richer and more valuable. Then you have all the more reason to protect your island.

The activity of protection and acquisition depends on the point of view that you are one isolated island that needs to be perpetuated and enhanced. Don't you spend most of your life either protecting or collecting? Even if you become spiritually oriented, you start collecting spiritual experiences! Collecting money or collecting essence is the same thing. You have the same attitude: you're afraid of losing it and you work at getting more. If you have an attitude of anxiety and fear of loss, the greed and the suffering will continue.

Let's look at the implications of this attitude more closely. Something happens and you get angry. What makes you get angry? Would you get angry if you didn't believe there was a self there to support and protect? What's the point of getting angry? You get angry only if you feel hurt, insulted, or you didn't get what you want. Someone is there who believes certain things about himself and has a particular self-image. If that self-image is frustrated, hurt or insulted, there is anger. Would there be anger if there were no self which thinks of itself in a certain way? Look at any suffering you've experienced: jealousy, anger, hatred, fear. Isn't that suffering dependent on the point of view that somebody is there being hurt? Doesn't the feeling of insult or humiliation mean there's someone there who has pride? Doesn't the feeling of frustration mean there is someone there who wants something and is not getting it?

Not only do you not see reality as it is, its beauty and its majesty and its grandeur, you are also hemmed in and restricted. Don't you spend hours and hours ruminating, thinking, proving or disproving that you're good enough or not good enough, as if there is somebody there who is supposed to be good enough? According to whose standards? Your own! Aren't you always thinking of what you're going to get for yourself?

What determines the content of your thoughts, of your heart, your emotions? What determines the content of your life? Isn't the biggest determining factor the point of view that there is a self there who is separate from everybody else and insecure, who needs to be protected and needs to collect things to satisfy its needs so it can continue living, continue being an island? You relate any experience you have at any given moment to a point of reference.

Whenever you judge your experience, aren't you relating it to a point of reference? Whenever you react emotionally aren't you depending on a point of reference? Even the fact that you're concerned about the suffering brought about by this point of reference is dependent upon that point of reference. "Oh, now I can see that I think I'm an island which I have to protect and this causes me suffering." Who's talking? Who's suffering? When we look closely at the situation, you will see that there is something we call our self which depends on a certain boundary and boundedness. We exist inside this boundary of our self with our identity; this is our universe.

Where did that universe come from? Isn't that universe with its blueprints, ideas, plans, dreams and preferences a product of your past? There is nothing new in it, nothing fresh. What you call your self, your sense of boundaries, your sense of identity has nothing to do with the present; it is a reaction to the past.

We're seeing some of the implications of the point of view of the ego believing in itself. This point of view is based on deficiency. Always. You may believe that you are open to new things, but are you really? The ego perspective is an insular and restricted point of view which doesn't allow for any fundamental change or fresh experiences. It does not allow existence itself.

As long as we relate experience to ourselves—even if the experience is a positive one—it will result in frustration and pain. If you believe you are a somebody having an experience, you will use that experience to enhance yourself, to make yourself feel better. This means that when you have a pleasurable experience, you're afraid of losing it and you want to repeat it. When you have a painful experience, you want to reject it, change it.

The point of view of having a self, an ego, is the same as the activity of reaction. Because of your past experiences, you are always reacting mentally and emotionally to your present experience. You don't just experience what is there.

When you look at a mountain, you do not see a mountain, you see what you think a mountain is and what you feel about the mountain. You do not let the mountain act on you; you act on it.

No doubt you're wondering, "Well, what can I do about it? What's to be done?" We need to investigate this question. When you ask, "Well, what are we going to do now?"—is that question related to you? Is it a reaction from the same island that we were just talking about? If you feel that something needs to be done, doesn't this depend on the point of view that things should be different and better? You want your island to be a little more comfortable, better arranged. But we're saying here that that's precisely the difficulty: we believe there's this island which needs to be supported and enhanced and improved.

It is possible to look at the situation, to be aware of it completely, to understand it without judging it, without thinking of changing it or desiring it to be different. We can explore without needing to protect a point of view or accumulate knowledge or experience a new experience. We can explore with no other motive than to understand.

The I, the ego, is engaged in continual activity: rejecting, wanting, justifying, judging, discriminating. This activity itself is suffering, and is the source of the point of view which believes in its separateness. As long as you are engaged in any desire to change things inside you, to want something to be different, you are coming from ego and identified with that point of view.

You cannot perceive reality as long as you are looking at the world from the perspective of the ego. To act from that point of view means to perpetuate it. The moment you think of change, of fundamental transformation, of enlightenment, you are speaking from the point of view of the ego. You think there is someone who is going to change, be enlightened and have all kinds of wonderful things. You want the island to become a paradise—lush and beautiful with all kinds of rivers and gardens full of fragrant flowers. You can't think any other way! If you believe in islands, no matter how rich and wonderful your island may be, you are bound to suffer fear and frustration.

Nothing I say about this can convince you that your ego point of view is the main source of your suffering. You have to observe it in yourself to see if it is true. Otherwise you will still be thinking that you'll get something out of what I've been talking about—that you'll be happier, more expanded, better at understanding.

This ego point of view is very subtle. It is so deep, disengaging from it is almost impossible. Most of the time you don't even want to disengage from it. You don't know what other point of view there is. "If I don't take what I want, I won't get what I need. This world is full of hungry wolves. If I don't look out for myself, I'm done for."

There are other points of view which are possible, more open, unbounded and with no sense of self. It is possible for reality to be seen not from one point, but globally. It is possible to live without relating all experience to one center and for human experience not to be bounded by that island, but for the whole universe to be its universe. It is also possible to see that the sense of boundaries and isolation depend on certain misunder-standings, beliefs and insecurities you want to cover up.

Although you believe in the island, it's also possible to see that the island is imaginary, fictitious. It does not exist in a real way. It doesn't exist in the way a mountain exists or the body exists. It doesn't exist in the way essence exists. It is a mental construction, made up of memories which form a point of view. It is possible to see this as a collection of tensions in the body which meet at one point. You look at the world from this point, this place of tension. It is possible to see that the whole island is really covering up something and that it exists so you don't fall into the ocean. You think you're trying to separate your-self from other islands, but you're really trying to separate yourself from the ocean—the universe itself. You might discover that this point of view is just a ploy to avoid inse-curities and fears which are the result of basic misunder-standings. It is possible to experience reality without taking a position about it, to be completely open about experience whether you are enjoying it or disliking it. If you look at yourself at this moment, objectively, you will see that you are taking a certain position within yourself about what I'm saying and what you are experiencing. You are judging: preferring or rejecting. It is possible to live without taking a position about your experience, without having continual commentaries on your experi-ence. It is possible to perceive and experience without reaction, without the mind or self responding. But this can only happen through understanding what you do, understanding how you are constantly taking positions with respect to your experience.

It is possible to look at a mountain and just see a mountain. It is possible to experience a painful feel-ing—sadness, hurt, jealousy—without having a point of view about it. This is an energizing experience which brings openness and peace, regardless of what the experience is.

It is possible to see that everything that happens is a creativity, is the process of life itself moving, changing, transforming. Suffering occurs from taking a position; a position is rigid and goes against life's movement and change.

It is possible to be an emptiness where you can experience someone completely because you become them completely. There is no position which gets in the way of the experience. When you have no point of view, you can look at a flower and know the flower completely, without reaction or judgment. This perspective where there is complete openness to things, without the rigidity of a point of view, is reality. This is the absence of rejection, judgment, suffering and restriction. This openness allows essence in all its manifestations.

It is possible to see that the reason you're suffering is that you're always filling your self with the activities of the positions you take. When this is happening you cannot experience things freshly, directly, purely. You even experience your body as heavy and sluggish. If you allow emptiness, your body can become light, rather than a hindrance or a boundary for your experience. Your body is your orientation in the physical universe but your experience does not have to be limited by its shape or contour.

You are basically an openness and a sensitivity which has no point of view, which is not restricted by any boundary of any kind—emotional, essential, physical or mental. When you allow yourself to be that openness and freedom, you will experience yourself as giving, as a flow of love.

The point of view of the ego is what stops love and the true abundance that flows like a fountain. The fountain isn't thinking of giving or not giving. The fountain is just there, flowing. A point of view, which is automatically a restriction, blocks the heart. The heart cannot pump its essential juices.

As long as you believe you are a separate person with boundaries, with the attitude of getting things and protecting your self, you will block love. Love destroys boundaries. Love has nothing to do with you or me. Love is just the activity of that creativity in that openness. Love is the outcome of non-restriction, of freedom. When the body and the mind are not restricted by that point of view, the harmony of the body and the mind will be expressed in a lovingness, an abundance. The natural movement of our being is to be in love. The expression of that freedom is love, goodness, sweetness, contentment. When there is no point of view, there is complete and real love. When love is present, there is no movement toward getting or protecting. Your body exists as a channel for that flow of love. Love will flow by itself. The openness and the love flowing through it will allow everything to happen the best way it can happen.

In this state of love, there is no sense of getting or keeping or even giving. There is no you and someone else. No islands. There's love and an emptiness, a whole universe. You are nothing but an individual expression of that love. When you see that you have a point of view and allow it to relax, let your mind relax, love will emerge spontaneously and you will see that you are not separate, you will experience directly that we are all individual expressions of the same thing, different parts of the same thing, of a unity and a wholeness. On the most basic level, that is how things really are. There is no separateness. The separateness is a belief you have which keeps you cut off from the natural outflow of love.

It is important to see that it will not work to try to acquire the freedom and loving abundance. It's not a matter of accumulation or of getting someplace. It is a matter of understanding the situation and of seeing that if you adhere to a point of view of acquiring, you stop the flow. The freedom and loving abundance will be there when you cease your acquisitive and defensive activity.

We are seeing that there is the point of view of ego which blocks openness and freedom, and the perspective of reality which is how things are, the natural order.

Now we will have questions.

Student: How do the ego fixations of the enneagram, the nine types, relate to what you've said about islands?

A.H. Almaas: They are just different types of islands.

S: I understand that, but you said that there are as many islands as there are people, and it seemed that maybe there are fewer islands.

AH: There are as many variations as people. We could put those variations into groupings. One of the groupings is the nine points on the enneagram. But even within one fixation there are all kinds of variations. No two people are the same. No two people are the same, but in another sense, everyone is the same. Basically all fixations operate from one perspective. There are nine types or fixations but they all come from one point of view—of acquiring things for the self, and defending that self. When you see that your focus on your self, your separateness, your preoccupation with your personal life, are all barriers against the natural order of reality, you become more willing to be open and loving. There is no threat then about being generous. You see that generosity is our nature. There is no loss in letting go of your point of view; there is tremendous gain—yet no self gains it. The gain is everyone's gain, the gain is for the universe. You will feel freedom, joy, fulfillment and happiness—but these feelings are not for you to possess, they are for the universe. Whenever any human being loses his point of view, the entire human race benefits. Ultimately, the work we do to understand our lives and our selves is not for us individually, but for the good of everyone, for the earth as a whole.

We are not separate. We are a network. Just as you have cells and organs in your body which cooperate to make a harmonious entity, all life on earth, all forms of life cooperate to make one body. Our individual health will contribute to the health of the whole. This is why the more open you are, the more willing you are to be loving and to serve. This comes from a recognition that we are one being. It's no longer a question of giving. It's a flow—a flow from one cell to another for the health and maintenance of the whole organism. To think in terms of giving is to think from the perspective of the ego, which is that someone is there giving and someone is there receiving—separate entities. It is not a giving but a circulation, and we are happiest and most alive when we are part of that natural circulation, without anything obstructing that circulation. When the ego has a point of view and works to maintain it, you put up a barrier, a dam. This blocks one little meridian of the earth.

S: Sometimes people attack me verbally. I know it's important to be able to defend myself against these attacks. How does this kind of defending fit in with what you've been talking about?

AH: Defending yourself is to defend against the superego, whether it is external or internal. The purpose of the superego is to preserve the ego's point of view. The superego ultimately stops you from seeing reality. Defending yourself is one method you use to help you look at things objectively and without fear. When you start learning how to defend yourself against the superego you can't help but think in terms of having a self to defend. Ultimately, what is actually defended is the openness, the understanding and the awareness. In time, we learn that understanding and awareness are the best defenses. When the awareness is complete, there is nothing to defend. Defending yourself is a kind of detour: you have to have a self before you can see you haven't got a self. You have to have a self before you can let go of it. When you have a scattered self, it's hard to let go of it. When you have a self that is depressed, scared, or fragmented in some way so that it can't handle reality, you're going to be very busy trying to protect it. You can't possibly allow the openness which would mean a loss of boundaries; it would be too scary. When you learn to defend yourself against attacks, you become stronger and you can allow the openness.

When you give or love selflessly, it means you are no longer bounded by a rigid point of view. It doesn't mean you stop existing as a person. Instead, you exist as an openness to experience, rather than as boundaries constructed by your mind. This is a very radical perspective compared to the ego's point of view.

We have lived all our lives from the point of view of ego. All our ideas, our dreams, our anxieties have developed from the perspective of having a self that needs to continue, a self dependent on particular boundaries.

We are being. We are essence. Being does not need boundaries and is not separate from the basic energy. It is true that physically we are separate from each other, we are not identical, we have different bodies. But on a fundamental level we are not separate: our bodies are nothing but expressions of the basic energy, of the basic consciousness. We are different waves of the same ocean.

If you see this, you cannot help but love. Love is not seen as a loss. Love is what there is. We usually think of love as a loss, a loss of ourself. It is a loss of boundaries that define this self. Love means you're not thinking of yourself as contrasted to somebody else.

S: If a person is really open, what is the effect on a person who's around him?

AH: This depends on the other person. Since love tends to erase boundaries and separation, a lot depends on the other person's awareness and point of view, and whether they need to defend their point of view or can allow openness. If love is present, the other person may feel threatened and strengthen his defenses.

In the long run, love tends to bring out openness in other people. However, for that to happen, there's a need for understanding creating the channels for the love to flow through. Without understanding, there's a blockage; love can't penetrate. There's an interplay between love and understanding. Love needs understanding to help dissolve barriers efficiently. Love is the basic energy that is flowing, and understanding channels it and sends it where it's needed.

S: What's your opinion on nuclear weapons?

AH: Not having a point of view does not mean you don't take action concerning things that happen in your life. It doesn't mean being passive about what is happening around you. If there is openness, that openness can allow spontaneous and positive action.

Someone asked the Dalai Lama—the religious and secular leader of the Tibetan people—about nuclear energy. He said there's nothing necessarily positive or negative about nuclear energy. What's important is the attitude we have toward it, and what we do with it, whether we take an ego point of view about it or an open view. The perspective will determine whether it's positive or negative, like anything else—the mountain, sunlight, money, sex, anything that exists. Nuclear energy can be used for the best of purposes or the worst depending on the point of view of those using it. Nuclear energy has potential for helping humanity. But if it's used from the point of view of ego which is protective, scared and greedy, that same energy can be used for power and destruction. Nuclear energy is not the problem. The problem is our point of view.

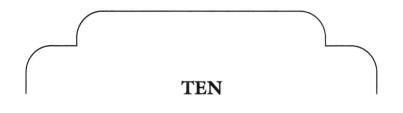

TEN

Love

Today we'll explore the meaning of a word that is misused more than any other word. Everyone uses it wrongly, so I tend not to use it at all, or I use it very specifically. The word which is so misused and misunderstood is "love."

If we really understood what the word meant, we would use it less, but there is a reason why we keep using it. We believe that we do know what it means. We like to think that we know what love is, and that when we say, "I love you," we really mean it.

Let's first explore the usual meaning, what people mean when they use the word "love." Then we can arrive at some understanding and appreciation of what the word "love" really refers to.

We generally use the word under certain circumstances and in specific situations. We reserve the word "love" for relationships between two people. We say that we feel love toward someone. We say, "I love you." There is always a specific other.

The usual use of the word "love" has to do with relationship, an intimate love relationship or other kinds of relationship. This is a very interesting assumption which everyone makes about love—that love exists in a relationship, is something you feel for someone or something, and that you give to someone or something. We will see as we go on that this assumption is the opposite of what love actually is.

Another common assumption about love is that it is experienced not only towards another, but towards a special other. You feel that it's okay to love your child, your husband or wife, but you don't think of loving just anybody. You don't think that you could or should feel love toward all the people driving down the freeway. "What does love have to do with those people?" you wonder. Love is special, you feel; it's only for particular people. In your mind, the people you love are important and no one else counts much. All those other people have nothing to do with your love. When you think of it this way, there are very few people that you love—just a few people, a few animals, your cat maybe, who you feel are very special. And because they're special to you, you love them.

This implies that you don't feel love very often. You feel love only when you are with those few special people, or when you are thinking about them. So love is for special people at certain times. It is not something that is there all the time, like air.

We have more assumptions about love. One is that you feel love for the other person only if he is being the way you believe he should be. You have certain conditions about how the other person should be, and then you can feel loving. If any of those conditions is not fulfilled, love disappears.

The first condition we have for love is that it occur within a relationship. The second condition is that the love be toward specific others in relationship. The third condition is that you love the special other only under specific conditions. The other person rarely fulfills all the conditions, and those conditions restrict the range of love.

What are our other assumptions about love? One is that love is an emotion, a feeling towards something or somebody. We believe love is an emotion like sadness, anger or jealousy. And we are concerned not only that we love the other person, but that he love us back. We are always concerned about getting love in return, and about getting enough.

Not only does our love require all kinds of conditions, our interest is typically not to love, but to get love, and you have all kinds of conditions about how that love should come, in what form, in what quantity and at what times. A woman says to her husband, "Don't say anything about love to me before 10 o'clock at night. Up until then I'm too busy talking to my friends. I have other things to do." The conditions are not just on our own love, but even on the love that comes from outside.

A basic factor here is the assumption of a relationship. There is a me and there is an other; there is love coming from me toward another person, or from the other person toward me, as if love is an object that can be thrown at someone. If you see love this way, there's not much difference between a person giving love to somebody and a cannon firing a cannonball into his belly. Then you complain that the other person doesn't appreciate your love.

You can see that you are not clear in your mind about what love is. When you say to someone, "I love you," what do you really mean? When you are passionately in love with someone and you tell him how much you love him, is that really love? What is involved in this feeling?

If you really look at the feeling, you may see that when you say, "Oh, I really love you! You're wonderful!" what you are really feeling is neediness. You want to eat the other person up. You don't want him to go away. That doesn't mean there is no love present, but what you are mainly experiencing is neediness.

When people say, "I love you," they are usually expressing not their love, but their need. When you are truly loving, you rarely think about love. A truly loving person is not focused on her love. She does not go around advertising her love—how much of it there is or how deep it is.

When you tell your friend, "I love you so much," don't you expect something back? Don't you want him to tell you, "I love you too"? Suppose you tell your friend, "I really love you so much," and your friend says, "I know." Is this all right with you? What will you feel? You want to receive some positive feedback. "Didn't I just tell you I love you? Why don't you put your arms around me?"

When you say to someone, "I love you," you usually mean a lot of different things, like, "Give me something, perceive me, see my love, see I am good, tell me you love me, put your arms around me," or even "don't bother me," and so forth.

Not only do you have all kinds of assumptions, preconceptions and ideas about what love is; even when you're feeling love, it is not necessarily love. Most of the time, when you say "love," the point is not to express love, but to express something else. But when love is truly there, it is expressed by its presence. You don't need to say it.

When you say, "I love you," it is usually some kind of advertisement, or commercial. You are selling something. It's like putting your money in a savings account so you'll have interest in the future. The more you tell your partner you love him, the more he is supposed to love you and the more you're supposed to get something back—if not now, then in the future.

I'm not saying that when you tell somebody, "I love you," there is no love at all. There might be love, or not. But even when love is there, you are also expressing something else. You might feel a little bit of love, and that love lets you feel your neediness; then the need is so big, you tell the other person, "I love you," and you feel that your love is huge, when what is really huge is your need. It might be a passionate need, a passionate longing, but you think it's your love which is passionate.

We're seeing that the usual understanding of love is that it happens in a relationship, in a specific, special relationship, and that love is felt under certain conditions. We're also seeing that what is felt is rarely love, but mostly need. It is a transaction or a wish for an exchange.

Let's try to understand in more detail what the word "love" means. What is the specific feeling, meaning and state of love? What are the conditions that allow love?

The first thing you need to know is that your personality or ego does not know how to love. It cannot love. When you say, "I love you," it is always a lie, because the person who says, "I" cannot love, and doesn't know what love is. The personality does not know how to love. The personality is the product of the lack of love, so how can it know love?

The personality is what you usually think is you, what you call "I," "myself." When you say, "I," it is a lie. "I" doesn't love. "I" doesn't know how to love. "I" is there because you don't know how to love. "I" is there from the beginning because of the loss of love.

The very existence of "I" is the absence of love, the blockage and distortion of love. The "I" knows how to need; the "I" does not know how to love. It is not possible.

What we call "I," our separate identity, is our self-image. Even if the self-image knows what love is, it does not have the love and cannot be a source of love. In fact, when there is love, love tends to melt away the "I." The "I" relaxes and gets out of the way.

Now that we have established that the "I," the self, doesn't love, we'll try to understand what love is exactly. We usually think of love as an emotion, a feeling. Emotions are products of the personality, and are directed toward somebody or something. The "I" feels anger, jealousy, sadness, dislike and liking, preferences, judgments. The "I" is the source of these feelings.

Since the ego cannot love, and emotions come from ego, love must not be an emotion. If love is not an emotion, what is it? Is it a thought, an action? Someone might say that love is an energy and that the love energy comes from your heart chakra and enters someone else's heart chakra like a laser beam—or enters his ear, or some other orifice.

To really know love, you must first of all know your self. By your self, I don't mean the "I"; I mean you must know your being, who you are separate from your label, from your name, from the feelings you have acquired throughout the years along with your self-image, and the other ideas you have about yourself.

To know yourself is to know who you are beyond those feelings and ideas. Who you really are has nothing to do with what happened to you in the past, and who you are exists regardless of your feelings, thoughts and opinions about yourself and regardless of anyone else's opinion about you. You must first know this if you are to know love.

When I talk about "knowing yourself," I mean to know your being, your essence. You must know what essence is, that essence is not an emotion, that your being is not a thought, not an idea, not a concept about yourself.

Essence is who you truly are. The question you want to answer is, "What is the Me that is intimately Me at the depth of the heart, the Me that has nothing to do with ideas and labels?" "I" doesn't know what love is because "I" is not your being. "I" is the label you learned, your identity tag. It's what Nasrudin calls your "balloon."

One day Nasrudin was talking to a friend before going to sleep. Before he lay down, he took a balloon and tied it to his big toe. His friend said, "Why are you going to sleep with a balloon tied to your big toe?" Nasrudin said, "I do it every night when I go to sleep." His friend asked, "Really? Why?" Nasrudin said, "That's how I know when I wake up the next morning that it's Me." So, when Nasrudin fell asleep, his friend took the balloon and tied it to his own toe. Nasrudin woke up the next morning and looked at the balloon and saw it tied to the other guy's toe. He shook him awake and said, "If you are me, then who am I?"

That's the "I," the identity tag, the balloon. That part is not your being; it's just a tag. It's important to have it; otherwise, the IRS can't track you, the Department of Motor Vehicles can't find you. You must have ID cards and credit cards so that you can drive a car. Things would be difficult without your balloon, your label. It has its uses.

That identity card, however, is not what loves. But you think that is who you are. After a while you forget, and you take your Mastercard to be you. The more plastic cards you own, the more important a person you are. People actually feel important with lots of cards. They open their wallet—"see how important I am?"

When I talk about "knowing oneself," I don't mean knowing that tag, that self-image. I don't mean knowing how you feel about your body or how you look, or if you're short or tall or angry or sad. Not these. I mean knowing your inner nature, your true nature. There is such a thing. It's what we call essence. When you recognize your true nature, your being, your essence, you will see it is Being, because it is. It is in the sense that it is an existence. It is not a reaction; it is not an emotion. An emotion is not an is-ness. An emotion is an activity, a charge and discharge pattern. Essence is there regardless of the charge or discharge. There is an existence, a being-ness that can be experienced, and that is you.

If you don't know this beingness, you can't know what love is because love has to do with your being, your essence. It has nothing to do with your personality, your emotions or your ideas, your self-concept, your self-image, your accomplishments, your preferences, your likes and dislikes, your relationships. These things have nothing to do with your beingness.

Your beingness is pure; it is not contaminated by any of those things. Your beingness is always pure, always present, always perfect. Its main quality is an is-ness, an existence, a beingness. The personality is an activity, a movement, always going one place or the other, always feeling something, thinking something, wanting something, desiring something. Essence is not like that.

Essence is just Being. You are. What you are has nothing to do with what you want, what you don't want, what you do or don't do. It is just there. You could be doing anything, and the Being is there, and that is you.

Some of you have experienced your essence and some have not. Knowing your essence is the primary, basic condition for knowing what love is. If you have not experienced essence, you cannot really know what love is, or you will be confused about love. Even if you have felt love, you have not been able to separate it from needs and emotions.

It is possible to experience love or essence while the personality is there, but if you never recognize essence, you won't be able to separate what is real from what is not. You will call it love when it is need or desire.

I don't say what many other teachers say, that as long as the personality is there, there is no love at all. I think that love can be there when the personality is there. Essence can be there when the personality is there. However, if you don't know what essence and personality are, you will not be able to see the pure element of love. When somebody is in love, there is usually some love, at least in the beginning. That is what opens the heart. Then you get off into the emotions and reactions and the dreams and the ideas and all that, and you think that's love.

The love is what opens in us. When we know ourselves and our nature, and we recognize our essence, then we see that love is actually also part of our essence. It is a way our beingness manifests itself. The love is also beingness. When you are experiencing love, love is who you are. It is not something you feel toward someone. Love is your beingness too, a certain aspect of your beingness, a certain facet of that being, manifested as love.

Love is an existence, not a reaction, not an activity. It is not a thought, or an emotion. Is is as substantial, as real as essence is, because it is essence. You cannot *have* love because you *are* love . Whenever you feel you have love, there is a contradiction. What is happening is that the "I," the ego, is saying, "I have essence." The Mastercard is saying, "I have a person." It's a credit card walking around saying, "I own this guy." That's what we mean when we say, "I have love." It's really the other way around. Your beingness has a tag.

The most basic thing about love is that love is beingness, essence, existence. When you experience love as a movement, a reaction, an emotion, a fantasy, an action, an idea—it is not love. Love can bring these things about, but love is more basic and more profound than any reaction. Your nature is not your identity tag. It is you, who you are. When love is there, then who you are is love.

I don't feel I love this, and this and this. That is not accurate. I feel I am love. Love is not something I have that I give to someone. Love is me. And love is more me than my body, more me than my feelings, more me than my thoughts. Love expresses itself through my body, my thoughts, my expressions, my actions. All these things are the outer wrappings for love. Love itself is something that is more me, more intimately me, more intimately my nature than any of those factors.

What is the implication of this insight? If love is our beingness, our essence, and the very substance of our soul, then what is going on when we have love only in a relationship? It means you are yourself only in certain relationships. If you say that love can exist only with specific others, you're saying, "I can be myself, my beingness only with specific others and only under certain conditions." The conditions of the personality will restrict love, will restrict you, and you're saying then that you can only be yourself under those conditions. If you say, "I only love this person," what does it mean? What are you saying about yourself?

To really see that love is beingness, is-ness, is not easy. You cannot understand it intellectually. The way to understand it is to experience it, to taste it, to be it. You will be able to understand its qualities only when you experience it. Love is not an idea or a concept. If you've never seen a coconut, never tasted a coconut, someone could explain to you the taste of a coconut forever, but you would never really know what coconut tastes like.

If you taste essence, you know it. If you don't taste it, you don't know it. Everything is like that. When people say essence or Being or love is something mysterious, it means they have never tasted it. It isn't any more mysterious than anything else.

To say that love is a beingness doesn't mean anything to someone who doesn't know what beingness is. Being is not an emotion. It does not even feel the way your body feels. Beingness means knowing that I am, that I exist as an is-ness, without reference to anything else. You know your body exists because you can feel it, see it, but that is not the way essence is. Essence exists not because you can feel it or see it. It is more intimate than that. The knowing of existence, the feeling of existence and the existence itself are all one thing.

This category of experience is not available to the personality. To know an atom, you look in the microscope and see its shape and color. If you were to know the atom the way essence is known, you would need to be the atom itself and know what the atom feels like. There is no true knowing the atom by looking at it.

As you can see, the beingness of essence is very far from emotional reactions, or something you give somebody. There is no somebody having something. The mode of knowingness, the mode of taste, of beingness and love doesn't have that kind of separation, which as we have seen is the only mode in which the personality functions—there is me knowing something, me experiencing my body, me having an emotion, me having an idea.

It is not that there is a me which has love; the love and the me are the same thing. I don't mean that they are two things intertwined—I mean they are the same thing. It is not that this finger has this finger. They are so intertwined that I know I have love, but I am not separate from love. It is one finger, and the finger says, "I am."

Essence has many manifestations. It can manifest as compassion, joy, peace, intelligence, emptiness, awakeness, or many other things. When essence manifests as peace, for instance, I and the peace are not two things. When essence manifests as love, we see that love is a certain specific mode of our beingness. It comes from a knowing, a relaxing into our beingness.

Love is actually more than one aspect of essence. When love is first discovered, one often feels it as a certain sweetness, a sweet presence which feels fluffy and light. This is one of the simplest and easiest aspects of love to experience, love which feels fluffy and pink.

Love is often experienced in this way in the beginning, as a sweet lightness, a softness and a gentleness that melts in you the way cotton candy melts. When someone says, "I love you," it is often the fluffy pink love they are experiencing. It feels like liking.

When you have discovered this loving aspect of essence, this sweetness, fluffiness and softness, you may begin to see the elements the ego attaches to love —need, wanting, desires and preferences. You may find that your personality lets you experience love only with certain people and only under certain conditions. This means that the love aspect of your beingness is connected to certain conditions from the past. Only under these conditions do you allow yourself to feel love.

Men often won't allow themselves to feel this kind of love because it doesn't feel masculine. They feel soft, more like a woman, more feminine. Some men say, "I don't want to feel this. This softness, this lightness is not manly." This is a condition the culture puts on love, that only women should feel this way. However, it has nothing to do with men or women. This kind of love is an aspect of our essence.

There are many different kinds of love. One is an aspect of love which has a melting quality, which we call merging love. It has to do with the loss of the boundaries between you and your environment; you experience merging with your environment. Your boundaries melt away, and you have no shields around you. You experience yourself as a delicateness, an exquisiteness that does not feel itself separate from anything else. This experience brings about a sense of contentment, and a deep letting go, a deep satisfaction. It feels like you are your own nourishment, and actually that you and the nourishment are the same.

This is the kind of love people want when they desire closeness or oneness with someone else. Dreams about togetherness, about community, about being One, about being inseparable lovers, are actually desires and hopes for this kind of love. This kind of love makes you feel merged with yourself and with everything else. There is an innate feeling of togetherness with everything in a sweet way. The sweetness of the feeling is like honey, but lighter and more delicate.

As all of you have observed in your work, the experience of essential aspects brings up the personality's issues regarding those particular aspects. In the realm of love, many different issues arise. Merging love brings up issues around closeness and separation. Issues around the fluffy love have to do with whether your love is rejected or accepted, whether somebody loves you or not, and whether they love you for who you are.

When you know your essence, you can allow yourself to experience merging love with another person; you don't feel the need for barriers between you and the other. When you feel your beingness and the beingness of the other, it is okay for them to become one beingness. When there is no issue of me and you, of boundaries and separation, then there is no issue of us as One. Merging love creates a state with no barriers. There are no barriers then between you and anyone or anything, between you and your body, your surroundings, your car, the whole universe. You feel you are sharing in everything, you are part of everything, melted with everything. Your heart is open and melting like butter.

This is a deeper aspect of who you are, a deeper realization of yourself. You begin to know yourself without reference to your body, your feelings or your environment. You are a depth. You look into the distance and you don't feel you are looking at the distance; you are the distance. You look up into the sky, into the clouds and you don't feel you are looking into the clouds. There is no distance between you and the clouds. You are the clouds. You are here and everywhere. Your boundaries are gone and the belief in boundaries is gone. They have melted away. This kind of love is one of the most difficult for people to experience in love relationships even though it is exactly what they say they want.

Most conflicts in love relationships are about merging love. "How close can I be with you? I don't want to be too close, but I don't want to be too far away either." Issues of closeness and distance will attempt to block merging love. When you are your beingness, it doesn't matter how close or how far you are. There is no need to set a boundary for your space because you don't have a particular space. That boundary is always overflowing, always melting away. Your boundary is like butter. When it comes close to the warmth of the other person, it just melts.

There is the sweet, fluffy kind of love, the merging and contented kind of love and then there is a third kind of love: passionate, powerful, consuming and ecstatic. You feel you've been taken by storm. Your mind is gone. You feel power and lustiness, passion and zest. You feel your whole being is burning like a flame and that flame is full, and that fullness is the love. You feel ecstasy, passion and no difference between desire, wanting, giving, receiving. It is all one consuming thing. I call it ecstatic, passionate love. This love is not only directed toward a person. It is again your beingness. You *are* the passion. It is true passion, not the passion of the emotions, which is fake passion. When you are passionately longing or passionately wanting, you are being your passionate self. But as true passionate love, you feel like a consuming force of life. When you look at life and existence, you're not wanting something from it, you simply appreciate it and love it passionately because life and existence are so beautiful. Beauty is a part of that passion. What ignites that passion is beauty, the exquisite, luminous beauty of existence. Everything and everybody is beautiful, and every occurrence is beautiful. You are everything, as manifestation of sheer, wonderful beauty. The more beauty you see, the more you burst with that passion. You love life. You want to love life because it is so wonderful, so beautiful, and you feel so strong about it. I call it "lion-hearted love." Your heart is courageous and forceful. It does not occur to you to wonder, "Is this person going to like me?" You have no worries. Your heart is so full that there is no room for doubt or fear. You appreciate what is there. You take life fully, completely.

All the aspects of love have some kind of sweetness with them. The sweetness of this love is exotic, like pomegranate, with a little bit of tartness to it. You feel strength and power. Passion is love with strength— strong sweetness, sweet strength. Your heart feels powerful, pulsing with life. There is a lust to this love, but not the lust of need. Rather, there is a lust and appreciation for life. You feel a complete involvement, complete participation in life, as if every atom is totally interested in participating, with nothing held back. Everything is delicious! You are eating up life, eating up yourself, eating up everybody. Everything is being consumed! You are lusty about life because life is so incredibly delicious and yummy.

The personality, of course, has its opinions about these things. The issues that arise around this kind of love are connected to the oedipal situation, the very early feelings you had as a young child. These feelings have to do with someone very specific—if you're a woman, you wanted your father, passionately; if you're a man, you wanted your mother, passionately. You wanted them passionately, body and soul. Their body was the most voluptuous, delicious, the most beautiful, desirable, yummy body in the world. And you carry that feeling of that deliciousness in your unconscious and wait for the right body to appear before you can re-experience the depth of that passion.

Do you remember what I've said about love? Love is our being. It is who we are. It is not a reaction or anything we give to someone. You can believe very deeply that you cannot feel this passion until the right kind of body appears, but that right kind of body might never appear. When you experience this passion, however, what you're really seeing is not the other person's body, but the fullness of your own being, the physicality of your being, the substantiality of your being. You passionately love these qualities in yourself, but you think that you see them outside yourself. Essentially, that desirable body you have in your mind, in the memory of that very early experience, is you. You are the deliciousness, the voluptuous presence. When you see this, then you are passionately in love, completely and passionately in love and consumed by your passion. When this feeling is available to you, you can feel it toward everyone and everything. It no longer needs to be specific or fit any requirements in your mind based on early experience. It is unrestricted, unbounded.

All our previous ideas about what love should be were the barriers. When you direct that passionate kind of love, that part of your beingness, toward what you perceive as a voluptuous body, you limit yourself to those ideas you had toward your mother or father when you were a very small child. But the voluptuousness is actually a reflection of who we are, an aspect of our essence.

All these aspects of essence have to do with the heart. I mentioned three that are specifically love. All manifestations of the heart, however, contain love in some form. Compassion, kindness, gentleness, accepting, allowing, graciousness, welcoming of experience and warmth are also love, or loving kindness, which is different from the three aspects I have discussed.

Love can manifest as joy, which is also sweet. Joy is very playful, light and happy. Love can also manifest as the aspect of fulfillment. When you feel your heart is full of nectar, when you feel your beingness is not only loving, it is fulfillment itself. When you experience yourself as a thick sweet nectar, then you are the nectar of Being. You are drinking yourself. This can be seen as love loving the action of love.

Contentment is an aspect of love, as is satisfaction. You don't experience the satisfaction. You are the satisfaction, a deep contentment. When you experience your heart or your essence as gratitude, you are not grateful for anything, you are the gratitude itself.

Fluffy love has a feeling of lightness and of liking someone or something; merging love has a feeling of giving and sharing with another person; passionate love has the feeling of whole-hearted participation in the world. Other kinds of love, such as fulfillment, satisfaction and gratitude, are different in that they have nothing to do with relationship, with other.

Not only are the heart qualities aspects of love, all essential aspects include love. There is no part of essence that is not loving. The action of any aspect of essence is always loving or in the service of love. Your strength is loving, your will is a loving will, the peace you experience is a loving peace, your joy is a loving joy, your intelligence is a loving intelligence. Love is a quality of all essence, although it is not always experienced as sweet.

Teachers in many traditions call all of essence love. They say that when you know yourself, you know you are love because essence as a whole is a loving presence. Seeing that all of essence has a loving quality and can only act lovingly will help us to understand another kind of love that I want to talk about.

All aspects of love can coexist with the personality, and the identity can be maintained, except in the presence of one particular aspect of love. This is called universal love, Christ love, or divine love. When our beingness manifests as universal love there is no personality. It is this love that spiritual teachers refer to when they say that as long as there is ego, there is no love. They are talking about universal love.

Universal means it is not restricted to you; it is not individual. When you feel universal love, there is no "I" that loves. Universal love is needed to melt the identity and self-centeredness. When you experience universal love or Christ love, you understand what love really is. Until then, all other qualities of love can be perceived as accomplishments, because the personality will claim them.

Finally, you will see that what gets in the way of love are not issues of liking and rejection, of merging and separation, of desire and passion, but the presence of the ego—the presence of the identity, what you call your self. You see that the real issue ultimately is you. You are in the way. To understand this is to understand the Christ love, the universal love which does not come from someone or go toward someone, but is an overflowing, a love which is the expression of abundance. It is still a sweetness and a presence, but more expanded.

What do I mean when I say the personality or the identity is the barrier? This is not easy to understand. To understand the barriers you must be genuinely dedicated in your desire to exist as that kind of lovingness. You have to be willing to give up everything, all your ideas, all your beliefs, all your accomplishments, all your self-image, all of what you think you want or dream. Only then can you know this most expanded kind of love. Issues of relationship do not exist within this perspective because there is no me and no you.

Most people will respond more to universal love than to other kinds of love. People are comfortable with it, because there is no you and no me in it, and thus the various issues around other aspects of love tend not to arise. There is more trust then, and less fear.

One of the main issues regarding this aspect is fear. It is fear that makes you feel that there is a you which needs to be protected, a you which needs to be enhanced. In the experience of universal love, there is nothing to be protected and nothing to be accumulated. There are no boundaries that separate the inside from the outside. The love is an ocean, and you are part of it, a drop of it or a channel for it.

When I say that the personality or the identity must move out of the way in order to experience universal love, I am not saying you have to reject your personality. If you reject your personality, the rejection causes separation and there is an absence of love. Universal love accepts everything, including the personality. It doesn't see the personality as a barrier, it sees the personality as a part of what is there. From the perspective of universal love, the personality is one fish swimming in the ocean. Suppose this fish happens to be grandiose and thinks it is more important than the other fishes. Universal love says, "If it wants to feel special and important, that's fine. What difference does it make?"

The personality is made up of the interaction of identity with boundaries. The sense of identity, who you think you are, has the feeling of you as separate from everyone else, the feeling of you as a separate entity: "This is me. I end here."

The sense of boundaries which isolates you is needed for a sense of personality and identity. You believe that you have to have the sense of being separate from everything else in order to be you; that if you didn't have a sense of yourself as separate from everything else, you would not exist or be able to function. This is a very deep belief.

The mind doesn't understand a state with no boundaries. You have always lived as if you are someone who is different from other people, and different from chairs and everything else. You don't know if it is possible to be a being, to be oneself and not have that sense of isolation. But when you experience yourself from the perspective of essence, you see that essence doesn't have that sense of boundary, doesn't isolate, doesn't feel it ends somewhere. This does not mean that you don't exist as you. You still exist as you. But the ego doesn't know this is possible.

To allow yourself not to have boundaries means to accept your aloneness. At the very core of our assumptions about reality, we think aloneness means separateness. But aloneness is not being separate. Aloneness means having no boundaries. How can this be? It is a paradox.

Aloneness means your personality is not there, that essence is on its own without personality. It is beingness without the label. When the label falls off, the balloon, the identity, starts floating away. Then you say, "Wait a minute. I don't want to be by myself. Bring my balloon back—and this time, make it bigger!" That personality, that balloon has a certain feeling to it—which we get from Mommy and Daddy.

As long as we have the personality, we believe that Mommy and Daddy are around and we are never alone.

You don't know what it is like to be alone. As long as your personality is there, your Mommy and Daddy are there. It's as simple as that. As long as any part of your personality is there, there is the memory of your Mommy and Daddy, of the past, of other people.

As long as your mind is active, full of thoughts, memories, ideas, preconceptions, you are not alone. You acquired these thoughts and memories from other people. The only thing you did not get from other people is an understanding of how things actually are now. Being alone means being without ideas and preconceptions, being present now, without relationship to the past or connection to anything or anybody else. Just you.

To be completely you means being alone. When this is experienced, it will bring very deep grief and sadness. You have to learn to say good-bye to everything you have loved—not just your Mommy and Daddy, your boyfriend and your cat, but to your feelings, your mind, your ideas. You are in love with all of these.

Letting go of them will feel like a great loss, even a death. It is not you who dies. What dies is everyone else. In the experience of ego death, you don't feel you are dying; you feel everybody else is dead. You feel you're all alone, totally alone.

You have lost a boundary which was constructed from past experiences. But this boundary never really existed! It was just a belief. When you experience reality as it is, there is no sense of boundaries or of being separate, of inside or outside. These are concepts you learned at a very early age in order to protect yourself. As a six-month old baby, when you felt some negativity, or discomfort, you pushed the bad feelings outside so that you wouldn't feel overwhelmed. That was the original need for the separateness.

When there is no mind, you are not thinking, not conceptualizing, not remembering. When you are in the now, there is no feeling of a you separate from something else. There is no sense in the first place that there is a me. There is One.

That feeling, that sense of boundary and separateness, is the personality itself. The presence of the personality is experienced as a boundary and that boundary is not different from ideas of the past.

When the personality is gone, you feel alone, because the boundaries—your ideas and memories—are your father and mother. The separateness is your memories of your mother and father, your relationship with them and all your past experiences which you're bringing into the present.

Your past experience separates you from the now. That separation from the now is a boundary around you like an eggshell. To let the boundaries go means accepting aloneness. When aloneness is accepted, there are no boundaries. What you perceive then is just lack of boundaries. This will be experienced as a newness, a rebirth.

You will see that there is an ocean with waves. You are a drop, but that drop does not have boundaries. It is a concentration of consciousness, and that consciousness is not separate from the rest. The whole of existence is a consciousness, and that consciousness is love. This love cannot be seen as long as there is a sense of boundary because that sense of boundary is a contradiction, a statement that this love does not exist.

The moment that boundary is gone, Mommy and Daddy are also gone, along with all your ideas, and you're afraid you're going to die. What you'll see then is love, a boundless and infinite presence of love. Not only are you love, you see love exists and that everything is love.

First the sense of boundaries needs to go. Then there is just an overflowing. You are a fountain of love in the middle of an ocean of love. A person who has no boundaries is a fountain of love in the middle of an ocean of love. The fountain is the source of love.

In addition to boundaries, there is another aspect of the personality that will go when universal love is realized. This is the identity, which is a sense of what it feels like inside, a certain taste, a certain quality. It's how you recognize yourself. The personality not only separates, it gives a sense of identification.

There is a sense of boundedness and a sense of identity. When you say "myself" you can recognize yourself. You have a certain quality, a certain flavor, a certain feeling. You believe that sense of identity, that air in the balloon with its helium, oxygen and nitrogen is you.

Your ideas, actions, desires, judgments, rejections, acceptances and preferences are all attached to this sense of identity. It's what you call your self, and it's what you are most attached to. You think, "That's me."

But if you are that, then you can't be anything else. You can't be essence, you can't be love, any kind of love. You can't be will, you can't be any of those as long as you are attached to that quality which you think is you.

Your identity is something you feel is constant, always there. You recognize yourself with it. When you know your flavor, what you believe makes you be you, then it is possible to let go of it. Then you don't have to be any particular way. As long as there is attachment to the self, to the identity, you don't allow what's really there to be there.

The barriers, the boundary and the sense of separateness are composed of all the experiences of the past. These experiences of the past form the base of a pyramid. The identity is the tip of the pyramid. The tip of the pyramid disappears when you start to see that the base of the pyramid is made up only of ideas in your mind.

When the identity and the separateness are gone, then it is possible to experience universal love, to understand reality as love, to understand God as love. Universal love is the basic energy of the universe. It is there all the time. When people say they want love, it's like the fish saying it's thirsty. You are swimming in love. You are a part of it. It's always there.

The sense of identity separates us and prevents our perception of the ocean. When the identity relaxes, what you experience is love, and no separation. Each of us is a wave of the same ocean. We are all connected on the most basic level. We are one.

It's not an issue of going back and forth, or getting anything. Love is an overflow; it is what is there, nourishing everybody. Without it, nothing would exist. But you cannot perceive this as long as you believe in the reality of boundaries and ego.

This is why we say that universal love cannot coexist with the ego. What is your cosmic identity? It is universal love, the feeling that "I am love."

Even the strongest memories you hold on to are actually vague reflections of the real thing, of the real cosmic universal identity which is universal love, Christ love.

In a sense, you are Christ, but not as Christ loving someone else. Christ said, "I and the Father are one." The Father is universal love. We are all Christ, but we choose instead to believe in ourselves as separate structures.

We see here that the true nature of love is not a matter of giving, it is a matter of being yourself. And this self is not you as different from another. It is everyone, it is everything. It is the actual goodness in life, the goodness that is everywhere, the nourishment. It is life, and the energy of life itself.

When the universal love is there, what happens to other aspects of essence? What happens to the fluffy love, the melting love, the passionate love, the fulfillment, satisfaction, gratitude? How is universal love connected to all these?

Universal love is conscious and loving at the same time. It is also known as universal consciousness or cosmic consciousness. Universal love is a unification of all aspects of essence. When you experience universal love, you understand the action of love. An action is loving when it has all aspects of essence. A loving action is a gentle action when gentleness is needed, a firm action when firmness is needed, a compassionate action when compassion is needed, yielding when yielding is needed. Whatever is needed is present—and in the correct balance—depending upon the situation.

This means that for us to operate from the perspective of universal love, all the essential aspects must be free, and available without blockage.

We see that the action of love is balanced and the manifestation of love is balanced. Whatever is needed is brought forth. Universal love has power, harmony and balance. The loving action is a balancing and harmonizing action. Universal love is mysterious: the mystery is that the abundance, the cosmic universal goodness is actually the expression and the radiance of the harmony of Being. The mystery is also that essence in all its aspects, can be present in a harmonious totality.

Universal love is an expression of the harmony of the totality. Everything is in harmony with everything else. Nothing is excluded. Your will is in harmony with your compassion. Your compassion is in harmony with your joy. Your joy is in harmony with your anger. Your anger is in harmony with your body. Your body is in harmony with your ego. Your ego is in harmony with other people. There is no conflict anywhere. Everything fits and functions as a togetherness, as a oneness.

That oneness is you.

That oneness is the true feeling of who you are. You are not the personality, or any particular aspect of essence. You are the whole thing, including emptiness and space, and you experience everything in complete harmony. When this happens, there is a sense of intimacy, an exquisite, personal intimacy, the feeling that you are you, with nothing excluded, nothing rejected. You also feel that you are both a person and a universal existence, that what is personal and what is universal are completely harmonious and can coexist.

When your whole organism is in harmony on all its levels, there is no conflict. The expression and radiance of that harmony is love. You become a channel of love, a manifestation of love. You feel completely yourself and not separate from anything.

It is possible to be you, completely you and not separate from the other at the same time. This is the action of love. The action of love is to unite, to reveal the connectedness. A loving person doesn't love you—a loving person is love. Love isn't given. It overflows. It's not even your love—it's everyone's love interacting. Love emanates from us like the scent from a rose.

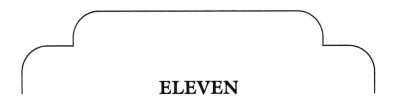

ELEVEN

Friend and Lover

Student: Would you be willing to talk about friend-ship, to define what a friend is?

A.H. Almaas: That's a nice question. It's a good idea to talk about friendship, about what a friend is.

Our usual understanding is that a friend is someone you spend time talking and gossiping with. What most friends do is get together and gossip and talk about their lives. When you feel like gossiping, you call a friend.

Another common perspective is that a friend is some-one who agrees with you most of the time about most people, about who's good and who's bad, whom you like or don't like. Also a friend is supposed to help you feel better about yourself when you're feeling miserable, by helping you patch up your holes. When you're feeling bad about yourself, your friend reminds you about your good qualities, and cheers you up.

A friend is also seen as someone who helps you through difficult times. If your girlfriend kicks you out of the house, your friend will give you a place to stay. If you go bankrupt, your friend will lend you money and his car. A friend helps you and supports you when you need it.

But more than anything else, a friend helps you not to feel lonely. Most of the time, most people seek a friend when they're feeling lonely. So if there is a friend around, you spend your time with your friend talking, doing things, going places. You're not alone. You have a friend, as we say.

A friend is also seen as different from an intimate companion; a friend is not like a lover or husband or wife. You can tell more about yourself to a friend than you can to an intimate partner. We typically talk about our husbands and wives to our friends. We can reveal certain parts of ourselves to friends but not to lovers. This is because a friend doesn't have the vested interest of your lover or spouse. You don't want to tell your lover everything. Your lover might get angry and refuse to sleep with you for weeks. It's easier to go to a friend and complain and explore what's happening, and the friend gives you support and you go back to your lover or your spouse, and you're refreshed, ready to go into it again, supported by your friend. You're not alone with your wife or your husband; your friend is there too, giving you a more balanced and objective perspective on your situation.

So this is the idea of a friend—that a friend is someone who, although she is not as intimate with you as a lover, is available to allow you to open a certain area of yourself, because she tends to be more objective, and not enmeshed in your situation.

People often trust a friend more than they trust an intimate relationship. It's a different kind of trust. You're not as vulnerable with a friend as you are in an intimate relationship. It's a different kind of relationship. Of course, for some people it's the other way around—that friends are not to be trusted.

S: I don't expect as much from a friend. I call up a friend and say, "Let's go to the movies," and if they tell me they can't make it, it's okay. But if my lover says she can't make it, I feel terrible. "What's the matter? Why don't you want to go with me?"

AH: Yes, we have more expectations from a lover. Many people treat a friend as someone who is sort of extra, someone you call on in times of need or difficulty. For most people, then, the primary relationship is with your sexual partner. A friend is second.

We typically see our friends as equal to us—equal and separate. We communicate on a more equal footing. In the intimate relationship, there is more attempt to control, and also more conflict. We're more enmeshed.

One of the main differences between friends and intimate companions is that there is less physical contact with a friend. The physical contact is an important part of the relationship with an intimate companion. That's what makes the whole difference between the two. The moment you have sexual contact with a friend, the friend is, in a sense, not a friend any more. The sense of the merging or the enmeshment with an intimate companion has to do with the physical contact, whereas with a friend, the merging isn't there because the physical contact isn't there.

So the relationship with an intimate companion is similar to the relationship that a baby has with its mother, whereas the relationship with a friend is more like the relationship of the older child with the father. There is less physical contact. Actually for a boy the friend is usually the father, and for a girl, the friend is typically the mother. And since the desire for the physical contact generally focuses on the parent of the opposite sex, friends tend to be of the same sex. If you're of the opposite sex, the possibility of the physical contact is stronger and when the physical contact happens, the friendship changes.

Let's explore these ideas of what a friend is, and try to understand them in terms of their origin. We will assume that all these characteristics of a friend are a reflection or an imitation of what a friend really is. Let's say that what we take to be a friend most of the time is an imitation which reminds us of a real friend, and the imitation is sometimes closer to the truth than other times.

We said at the beginning that a friend is someone you talk and gossip with. What is gossiping? Isn't it a kind of communication? Talking with someone helps you know who you are. A friend is someone you express yourself with in a way that will make you aware of what's really happening with you in your life. Gossip is an imitation of true communication.

True communication is concerned with truth and understanding. It is a dialogue in which you become more aware of yourself and develop new understanding. That understanding brings about a release and an expansion.

If you are gossiping with a friend, you are hardly concerned with truth and understanding. Just the opposite! You are usually gossiping to distract yourself and avoid the truth, to avoid understanding. You are trying not to feel who you are.

Now what's the point of that? People get together with friends to distract themselves. Why? Why do they want to distract themselves? Because they don't want to experience pain, and they don't want to experience their conflicts. They don't want to experience the fears, the insecurities, any of the unpleasant feelings.

Now the gossiping mode of friendship is an imitation, whereas the true friend is someone who will help you deal with your pain, conflicts or fears so they can become more tolerable. The true friend will help you—not to cover up your feelings but to uncover them, so you can understand and release them.

Of course, true communication sometimes does happen between friends, and that's what determines what a real friend is—what a good friend is.

What else did we say friendship is?

S: Something about companionship. Somebody to pass the time with.

AH: Yes, the issue of loneliness. Right. You spend time with a friend so that you won't feel lonely, and you won't feel alone. That's a very important thing about a friend. In fact, most people spend a lot of time with friends, so that they won't feel lonely. So a friend is there to help you get over your loneliness—to deal with your loneliness by not feeling it any more. Again, the function of the friend is to fill a certain hole.

A true friend is someone who does not help you to avoid your loneliness but who helps you to deal with it. A real friend is someone who actually makes it easier for you to be alone. A true friend does not help you avoid feeling your aloneness, but helps you to feel and accept your aloneness. In fact, a friend is someone you can be really alone with more easily, in a sense, than in an intimate relationship.

It is harder to be alone with an intimate companion or partner because of the merging kind of connection. So a friend is someone who you can be with and also feel alone, and be happy feeling alone.

By "alone" I do not mean physically isolated. If I were going to define "friend" for myself, it would be someone with whom I can be alone. For me, the most real way of looking at a friend is somebody with whom I can be totally alone and be happy in being alone.

A real friend is someone who leaves you alone, who doesn't bother you, who doesn't impose his or her opinions on you, or give you advice. A friend doesn't tell you what's right or wrong. A friend is someone who not only leaves you alone but actively supports you to be alone, to be yourself. To be alone means to be yourself completely.

Leaving someone alone means not trying to manipulate them, not trying to control them, not trying to make them one way or another, not trying to make them respond in one way or another. When a friend leaves you alone, that friend is with you as an emptiness, in a sense, as an acceptance. This doesn't mean encouraging your indulgences or your self-hatred. If your friends encourage your indulgences and your hating yourself and your gossip and all that, they're not leaving you alone, they're helping you not to be alone. They're helping you to be fake. If you're with friends and you start gossiping they'll tell you they really don't want to talk about that.

We're exploring the nature of a real friend by considering the usual ways of looking at friendship. We think of a friend as someone who gives advice, assurance and support. Right? What is advice? What's advice for? What are we doing when we give someone advice?

S: To help them see something.

AH: Well, advice is not really to help somebody see something. Advice is when you tell someone what's the best thing for them to do. "Well, it's better not to argue with your wife. I remember when I argued with my wife, it got really bad. It's better not to say anything back to her." That's advice, right? Advice is essentially telling the person how to be, and ways to behave that will supposedly help him in his life.

Giving advice is an imitation of a function of a true friend. A real friend will not give you advice because advice does not help understanding, does not resolve anything, does not bring clarity. A true friend will help you arrive at insight about the situation, so that you yourself find out what's the best thing to do. So a friend is there, is present, to help you understand, to expose what is there in yourself and thus to understand what the situation is, why you are behaving in certain ways and why the situation is as it is. When you understand it, naturally you will know what is the best thing to do.

A friend does not give his own opinion and experience, and impose it on you. A friend helps you find your own solution. Another person's opinion of what you should do might not be appropriate for you. Who knows? It might be true that it's better not to argue with your wife, but not all wives are the same. With some wives it's better to argue. It depends on what's happening. What year of the marriage is it? Is it the honeymoon or is it the third year or the seventh year? What's your wife like? All these things have to be taken into consideration. The point here is not manipulation, but true consideration of the uniqueness of the other and the situation. A friend does not support your manipulations of another, but supports what is real, what is respectful of the reality of the situation.

A friend is someone who is there to help you understand yourself, to help you know yourself, and is there in a way that allows you and supports you to be yourself, and thus to be alone. A friend doesn't push you one way or another according to his own opinions. He might push you sometimes, but only to understand something. A friend might be angry with you if you're doing something to hurt yourself, or being unreal. A good friend will get mad, will get really furious sometimes if you're doing something that is not conducive to your health. A good friend will also be very happy when you are happy. When you do something that is good for you, when you expand, or when something wonderful happens in your life, your friend is full of joy for you.

At the same time, when you're hurting, or having difficult times, a friend is there—not so that you won't feel the hurt, but help you to take it, to tolerate it. A friend is a compassionate person.

When you're happy, the friend is full of joy, and when you're hurting, the friend is full of compassion. The joy is a celebration for your happiness and the compassion is a healing acceptance that helps you to accept your hurt and learn from it and grow. And from that growth there will again be joy and celebration.

A true friend is someone who is always available whenever you truly need him, available one hundred per cent of the time. And he's available with compassion, joy, love, acceptance, truth and support, without expecting anything back. A real friend is compassionate when you're hurting and joyful when you're happy because he loves you. A friend loves you not because you agree with him but because you are real, because you are true to yourself.

A true friend doesn't support you in gossip, in self-destructive tendencies or in falsehood, but supports the truth in you. The real friend is support for truth.

Whenever there is a touching of truth in you, the friend is happy. If you're hurting, a friend is compassionate, kind. If you happen to be angry because you're hurting, a friend is even more compassionate. The friend has no opinion about you. The friend has no prejudice about you. The friend sees you just the way you are. So the friend is completely objective, with no emotional bias of any sort. A friend is someone who can see you exactly the way you are at the moment and who is spacious enough and generous enough to allow you to be just that.

That's why people like friendship: because a friend is somebody with whom you can be yourself. You don't have to pretend, or put up a façade. You can be completely who you are; that is the true function of a friend.

A friend is always available to help. But what is the help for? The help is for you to be more yourself because the more you are yourself, the happier you are and the more you love yourself.

If the true friend helps you to see the truth and you don't act on it, the true friend is even more compassionate. The true friend can see why you're not following that insight; she can see the hurt that you don't see, and the fears that you don't see. She doesn't have the judgments about how you feel. She doesn't think it's shameful to feel hurt, or that it's bad to feel scared. When she sees you are feeling hurt or scared, your friend's heart is full of compassion and kindness. The more you reject yourself, the more kindness the friend has. Even if you reject the friend, the friend is still compassionate. If you reject the friend because you want to protect yourself against hurt, against fear, the friend cannot help but be more kind.

The friend is someone you can trust. And why do you trust the friend? You trust the friend because the friend has no opinions about you, has no prejudices about you, has no judgments or criticisms about you. The friend sees you the way you are, all the good and the bad, and only loves you, regardless of how you are.

When you're screwing up, the friend becomes firm, doesn't let you indulge, doesn't judge you for it, and will just tell you you're being a screwball. He waits for the time when you will listen. He waits for the right moment for you to see.

A true friend is firm when firmness is needed, is loving when love is needed, is understanding when understanding is needed. He helps you to see what's required—strength, support, clarity, or kindness and love, and helps you see those parts of yourself that you need in the situation. A true friend is someone you could be happy with by being the truth of who you are. If you're being false, the friend will just show you you're being false, not agree or disagree. Friendship has nothing to do with agreements or disagreements. Friendship has to do with understanding and truth, joy in the truth.

S: It sounds like a true friend is the definition of a teacher.

AH: It's the other way around. A real teacher is a true friend. What you need is a true friend, not a teacher. A teacher is generally understood to be someone who tells you how things are. We think a teacher sits there and tells us how things are, what we should do. But that is not what a real teacher does and not what a true friend does. A friend doesn't tell you how things are. A friend guides you so that you yourself can see how things are. That is a real teacher.

We are seeing here the relationship between a teacher and a friend. Ultimately, a teacher is a friend. A real teacher is simply one expression of a friend. Friendship is a more thoroughgoing relationship than that with a teacher.

You can be your own best friend, your own best teacher. You can have your own friend inside you, your most intimate friend who is with you all the time. What we call a friend is simply the external representation of a certain part of us which can do all the things that we want from a friend.

It is good to have an external friend. Your friend is a representative of your inner friend, a reminder and reflection of that part of you. And for you to be a friend means to be that part of you with someone else.

If you are really being a friend, you are kind when kindness is needed, you are happy when there is something to celebrate. You are always available for support, for love and for clarity in the service of truth. You're always there to help your friends to be themselves. You are objective about the situation; you're not acting according to your beliefs, your opinions or your emotional reactions to the person. You really see what's there, completely, clearly, objectively. And you respond appropriately.

If you are a friend, you leave the other person alone. You don't bother her, you don't judge her, you don't do anything. And you are there only when she needs you. If you're not needed you don't have to be there. And you don't feel rejected, you don't feel hurt, none of that business. That has nothing to do with being a friend.

A friend is someone who shows you yourself like a pure mirror, a pure mirror that changes color. It is the green of compassion when you're hurting; it is the bright yellow of joy when you're happy. A friend is not heavy-handed, but very light. The friend is always waiting to be invited, not for himself, but whenever he is invited he is present. He doesn't intrude, even if you're being a schmuck. The friend will be there only if you invite him. He is gentle and unobtrusive, and doesn't need or ask for any reward or compliment from you.

S: Would you talk about how attachment affects friendship?

AH: If you're attached you can't be a friend—not completely. Attachment will prevent your being objective, seeing what is really there, and what is needed. Attachment will make you prejudiced. That's why it is hard to be friends in intimate relationships. Objectivity goes out the window. Objectivity doesn't generally exist in the bedroom. When you enter the bedroom, you leave your objectivity outside.

S: What is the role of intimacy, an intimate relationship?

AH: First of all, an intimate relationship needs the attitude of a friend. An intimate relationship that has no friendship in it will become difficult in time, become mucky.

An intimate relationship is basically a love relationship. An intimate person is a lover. Supposedly the person you sleep with is someone you love. This is different from a friend. The love that exists in the bedroom is not the same thing as the love that exists between friends who are going swimming together, or whatever. The pleasures are different, and the involvement is different. There is more sharing, more interconnection.

A friend is more like a mirror reflection, a guidance and a support, while a lover is someone you enjoy. With a lover you are yourself in a specific way—you are more your heart. When you are being a friend there is more objectivity, lightness, and delicacy.

When you are a lover, a true lover, all those qualities exist as the space that allows the heart. In that objectivity, in that generosity, in that openness, in that acceptance, something else becomes possible. It becomes possible to lose yourself, to lose your head, to be just the heart, just the love, just the juice, the sweetness, the song.

From that objectivity, that generosity, that openness, comes the space actually needed for another part of you, a part of you that has to do with intimacy. It is a particular intimacy, the intimacy of love. And the intimacy of love is an intimacy in which you lose yourself.

You lose yourself not in the sense that you give yourself up or sacrifice yourself, but in the sense that you melt. You don't melt with a friend; you're full of joy with a friend. With a lover you melt; you are a melting, a sweetness, a nectar. You are a song in that emptiness and objectivity and generosity.

With a lover it's not a matter of being objective. It's not a matter of seeing or finding or understanding the truth. With a lover it's not a matter of being kind. With a lover it is a matter of being. You are the truth, you are the love, you are the life.

The lover is another part of you just as the friend is part of you. How? The lover is a part of you that is a source of delight. The lover is a part of you that is drunk with love, the part of you that is truthful not because it is objective, but because it has lost itself. It has lost the part of itself that makes judgments and reacts. That part is melted. It is gone.

There is truth and there is joy. There is also a sense of fullness and ecstacy, a sense of bliss and passion, and a sense of melting and sweetness.

With a lover you are a drink, a delightful drink. With a lover you are a happy song. You want to be with a lover not to talk about anything, but to disappear. You don't want to communicate; no, you want to be completely gone. It is not a matter of dialogue; there is no dialogue. There is oneness.

In the realm of the heart, there is no separation. That's why attachment and enmeshment are actually fake; they substitute for and imitate the real love situation.

In the real love situation, all the windows are opened— there are no protections, no attempt at protection, there is no holding back. It is not a question of being fully present; you're so present that you're gone. You are just a sweetness. The windows and the doors are so opened that there is no you and other. There is just one; the one is sweetness, love and appreciation. There's a playfulness; two hearts are singing in one voice.

With your beloved you are truthful, you are completely truthful, not by being objective, but by being completely surrendered. You're not trying to pretend anything, present anything, hold back anything, protect anything, control anything. You're a song, an uncontrollable sweetness—a fragrance.

This is another part of you. The friend is part of you and the lover is part of you. The lover and the friend can both be there together as one. When the lover and the friend are one, then the love and the juiciness are light, delicate, and refined.

When you're a friend and lover at the same time, you disappear, you're gone—you are a song. But that song is so delicate, so refined because it is objective at the same time that it is sweet. It's not like the mind is gone; it's more like the head and the heart are one. There is absolute clarity and that clarity itself is very sweet!

This is a rare combination for people. We usually separate the two. It's easier. However it is possible to be both.

When you are lovers and friends at the same time, you are not only two rivers merging, you are two crystalline rivers merging. There's a freshness, clarity, delicacy. The tenderness is very tender; at the time it is intense, and that intensity is delicacy.

The intense sweetness has a sharpness. The sweetness is so intense it is shattering. The sweetness doesn't only melt you, it shatters you. You become a sugar cube, a rainbow, a colored sugar cube.

Let's say more about the lover. What is it to be a lover?

The lover is supportive, kind, objective, joyful, gentle. The lover is the same thing as the friend, except that now all these qualities have a sweetness to them.

Love is the realm of the heart and the intimacy has to do with the heart. The heart has a crazy quality to it, a mad, drunken quality. There is a sense of a total involvement. There is no withholding of anything. Everything is there in the pot; everything is melted. Everyone is looking for that kind of love. "If I just fell in love with the right person I could be all that, I could be all myself, all myself as a sweetness." You believe this part of you can come out only at certain times, especially with the energetic help of sex to allow it to happen, to allow this part of your heart. You can be this way with someone else—but it is also a part of you. You can be this way unconditionally, whether there is another person to love or not.

When you are the lover, your kindness tastes sweet like lime candy; your peace tastes sweet like licorice; your joy tastes sweet like lemon drops; your truth tastes sweet like sugar cubes.

You are beyond the categories of the mind. You know and you are and you feel all in the same action, the same moment.

I think the best way to describe an intimate love relationship is that you melt, you melt into a river of sweetness.

Oneness is not a matter of giving or getting. Oneness is not a matter of understanding or being, not a matter of self or other. It's not a matter of compassion or love, love or understanding. It's all one thing. Everything is love.

You are so full of sweetness, you're bursting. Sweetness is coming out of your pores—you can't help it. You're melting all over the place, not because you want to give something to someone, not because you're loving, but because the heart is love. The heart is the abundance, the overflowing fountain itself, the substance of love itself. The expression of the heart is pleasure, and then life is always a celebration.

Love is really nothing but a synthesis, the union of truth and pleasure. When there is truth, when you are the truth, when you are the pleasure—together at the same time—then you are love. When truth is sweet, it is love. When pleasure is true it is love. Love has both the pleasure and the truth. In love there's no separation between truth and pleasure. People often ask, "Shall I go for truth or for what feels good?" Right? In the stories, the answer is, "Go for truth." Spiritual teachers say, "Yes, go for the truth. Pleasure is not that important—it'll come as a result."

The lover says, "I don't choose. Who am I to choose between truth and pleasure? There's no difference at all. When I am the truth I am absolute pleasure. When I am really feeling pleasure, when I am the pleasure, I am truth. In both cases I am the sweetness of love."

The heart has everything in it—the mind and the body. It is more of a totality than anything else. When you are the lover, all of you is there. You contact at all levels of your being; you share everything. If you feel you have to protect yourself, separate yourself, have something that is you, but not the other, that the other can't share with you, you're not being a lover. As a lover there is nothing to protect. There is nothing to protect, nothing to impose, nothing to give, nothing to hide. There are no decisions about anything; the mind isn't there.

As a lover, you're vulnerable; you're without protection, barriers, boundaries. There's no holding back, no closed doors, no closed windows.

As a lover, you don't have an issue of trust or no trust. To need to trust means you have not disappeared. The trust is implicit. The trust exists in the space around the friendship. The friendship is the trust and allows the openness, the emptiness, the peacefulness, the objectivity, the generosity, that is needed to be the space for the heart to open. Because you trust the friendship, you can melt. The trust is the friendship and the love grows out of it. Love is the fountain that flows out in the middle of the trust.

Beyond trust or no trust is the state of complete abandon. It's the love of the heart when you are at your source, before you have known yourself as separate from everything else. When you're a lover, you're a sweetness that doesn't think of itself. You are not concerned about being careful or cautious; you don't wonder if you're going to say the wrong thing.

The love becomes so intoxicating that you're completely drunk. You're so drunk you don't think about what you should say or not say. Whatever can happen happens. You don't know what will happen. You're drunk and that drunkenness is the love—the love is the drink.

You are being yourself, being who you are. You are being your heart with a personal aspect to it. The lover is the universal person, someone who is universal, objective, and intimately personal.

When you are a lover, you are personal, but you have no boundaries that separate you from your lover. A lover is someone who is personal with God, personal with Being, with essence. The only way you could be personal with God is through love—by being a lover. This is the only way. And that is the true essence of what a lover is—being personal with the universal.

You can be friends and be impersonal, but you cannot be loving and be impersonal. If you are loving, you are personal. To be a lover is to be personal with the totality, to be in communion with the universal. That is why there are no boundaries with love, no separateness. You cannot be rigidly separate from your lover, because being a lover means to be personal with no boundaries, no holding back, no closed doors. That's what it means to disappear, to melt—to be personal with everything. To be personal with God, which is the universal.

It's a difficult concept to grasp. The mind can't grasp it. It doesn't make sense. We are saying that two categories that don't go together actually exist inseparably in the lover; it defies all rules of logic. "I've never experienced anything like that. It's not possible." But love makes it possible. You could be completely in love with the universal, with everything, with the totality. Then you are a true lover.

A lover is ultimately the synthesis, unification and integration of the personal and the universal. There is no longer myself distinct from everything else. Myself and everything are the same thing. I don't love my lover because I think my lover is wonderful; I love her because I do not see any difference between me and my lover. When I look at my lover I see love. When I look at myself, I see love. Love melts the boundaries. If you are a true lover, you do not have separate boundaries.

The friend is the true mind and the lover is the true heart. So when I talk about the lover, I'm actually not restricting it to intimate love relationships. The lover is a part of you. Because of our human situation, we connect intimate love relationships with sex. But the lover is a part of you, just as a friend is a part of you.

When I say the lover is drunk, I don't mean unconscious. The drunkenness of love is not the same thing as the drunkenness of alcohol. I use the word drunk to mean that your usual intellect is not there. But this doesn't mean that there is no awareness, no clarity, no presence. The lover is really present. When you first fall in love, you know how aware you are. When you're really a lover, you are very aware of what's happening. You notice the slightest movements of your beloved, the slightest changes. You are acutely aware of him. Your beloved turns his head and you're aware of it, and why. He gets hungry and before he says anything you've brought food. Before the beloved says, "My back hurts," you're massaging his back. You start making plans for a trip to Hawaii and you don't know why. It turns out your beloved really needs a vacation. The lover is very sensitive and very aware.

The drunkenness is not unconsciousness. Your head is completely gone and completely empty. You just see what is there through your heart. Your heart has its own eye which sees and is sensitive. You please your beloved because it pleases you. When your beloved hurts, you hurt; when your beloved is happy, you're happy. There's no difference, no separation. You're sensitive and aware because there are no boundaries.

There's no difference between you and your lover. And the lover exists in you. In love relationships we are looking for the lover in ourselves. We want to be that open heart. We have all kinds of preconceptions and misconceptions about what it means, and these ideas prevent us from being, really being, the lover.

The lover is the one who is celebrating existence. The celebration is the pleasure that is the external manifestation of the lover. The life of the lover is an ongoing love affair with the world and everything in it. You love your beloved, you love life, other people, truth, understanding—everything—sometimes with passion, sometimes with gentleness or with sweetness. You are always in love. There is no one object for your love. You embrace it all. The moment love is restricted to one person or thing, it is limited and diminished. The lover is in love with everything all the time. You look up at a small white cloud, you feel dizzy. It starts raining and you are enchanted. A car goes by and you are thrilled. A lover really is mad in a sense. She experiences no barriers, no partitions, no holding back, no doubts.

A lover is someone who is completely involved in existence, completely participating; someone who is not trying to get anywhere—she's already there! The lover is someone who is just loving and enjoying what is there at every minute.

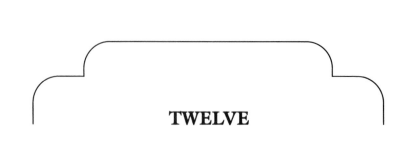

TWELVE

Being Oneself

Today we will explore something very mysterious. When a person becomes aware of him or herself, it is a mysterious thing; but it is mysterious only when we genuinely and closely try to understand it. If we don't question it, we think it is obvious; but when we question it, we discover that we really don't know what we are looking for. This mystery is what is called "being oneself."

What does it mean to be oneself? Everyone says he wants to be himself. "I want to be myself and express myself. I want to be me." The desire to be oneself is a very, very deep concern. In fact, most people feel it's hard to be themselves most of the time. Even when they are alone they are thinking, "I can't be myself." People talk about wanting to be themselves as if they know what that means. When someone says, "I'm not myself around my mother or my boss," it sounds as if they actually know what it is to be themselves. But the most important part of the problem here is not the presence of the mother or the boss, but the fact that one doesn't know what it is to be oneself. What is that experience, to be oneself? How will you know when you are being yourself? We go around feeling that we can't be ourselves, or wanting to be ourselves, or to assert ourselves, or to express ourselves. But what is being oneself? Notice the way I have phrased the issue. I'm not asking, "What is the self?" I'm asking, "What is it to be oneself?" These are two different issues. It is not what is the self, but what is it to be. It is the question of being that is a mystery.

The more mysterious something is, the more people take for granted that they understand it. The question of being oneself is such a mystery that most people believe they already know what it is to be oneself.

There are two parts to our question of what it is to be oneself: to be, and to be oneself. If you read the literature from many different traditions and teachers, you will see that they keep saying there is no self, but they also refer to being oneself. They say you need to be free from yourself, but at the same time they also say that you have to be yourself. How can that be? How can there be no self, but at the same time you need to become yourself? This is usually not explained. Of course, we often do not think to ask this question. The precise understanding of what it is to be oneself is not a simple one. We could even be free from the self, from the ego, and still not know what it is to be oneself.

So what is yourself? Are you being yourself when you're expressing anger? Or, are you yourself when you're expressing love, or when you're letting yourself be sad? Are you yourself when you do what you want to do?

That's another way people think they're going to be themselves—by doing or accomplishing what they believe they want. In fact, most people think they are being themselves by expressing a feeling, an idea, or an action. But we are trying to find out what it is "to be oneself," not "to do oneself" or "to express oneself."

According to my perception, it is this lack of understanding, the ignorance of what it is to be oneself, that is the main reason why people do not expand. It is why people do not develop in a real way; why people continue having the same issues, problems and difficulties. To truly develop means first you need to be yourself, and that your self will develop. If you are being something else, that might develop, but it's not you. People talk about self-development, but who is there who is going to develop? If you don't know what it is to be yourself, what is developing? You can take self-development classes, self-assertion classes, and develop something, but who says that's yourself? You can develop capacities, abilities, perceptions, experiences, and ideas if you work at it. But that doesn't mean you are developing yourself.

Many people go to very deep places, and have very high and refined experiences and insights, without knowing what it is to be oneself. Even when people really work on themselves, they are usually taking a detour. They get to states of being very open, very loving, very compassionate, even universal, without ever knowing what it is to be oneself. Although it might be wonderful, their experience becomes very limited, very restricted. The only way we can experience all that is possible for a human being is to be ourselves. If we are not ourselves, any other development is only a sector of human experience. To be a complete human being, to be a totality and experience wholeness, to be able to experience all possibilities and all potential for a human being, first we need to be ourselves.

When a person learns what it is to be oneself, the process of inner development, realization and understanding of truth involves continual discovery and expansion, with surprises and celebrations during the whole process. There is no end to the exploration and discoveries. Many of you can feel a very deep yearning, a subtle flame, a longing for that true life—to live our life as a continual celebration and freshness. In some part of us we know this is possible, and that it is the way life should be. If we don't live this way, there is always a feeling of incompleteness.

The understanding of what it is to be oneself unifies the spiritual and the mundane. It unifies the teachings of people like Christ and Buddha with the yearning of the ordinary person. The enlightened masters and teachers talk about renouncing the world, about being free of ego, and about their desire to live a true life. But an ordinary person is always wanting such things as pleasure and the fulfillment of his desire. We want the experiences of the physical world.

Why do we have all these desires and dreams? If there is no such thing as a life of abundance and celebration in a personal, ordinary way why do we desire them? These desires must come from somewhere. There must be some truth to both the universal spiritual teachings and the personal longing experienced by the majority of people. There must be something which unifies these so that they are not in contradiction. And to really make that unification, not theoretically or mentally but experientially, to see the two as one, is the door to knowing what it is to be oneself. Without this unification of spiritual and personal, even cosmic and divine experience lacks the aspect of celebration.

People who are oriented toward the impersonal, universal spiritual life have a certain misunderstanding. It's true that to forget about your personal life, to forget about yourself and become a monk or nun, can lead to liberation and enlightenment. But is that why we have a life? Are we supposed to abandon our life on earth to go somewhere else? The majority of humanity rejects this path, and continues to seek happiness and fulfillment here, in this life. So even though it's not possible to have a fulfilled life the way most people try to get it, there is something very deep and true in that striving for personal fulfillment. In that yearning there is a seed of understanding that all of this life, including the universal and divine, is for us. Why are we here if the abundance is not our lot in a personal life, if we are not going to enjoy it? The way the ego goes about it doesn't work, but the original impulse is not false. This is a mystery that is rarely understood.

Most people in spiritual work assume that the ego is a problem and consequently miss the truth that the ego can reveal, because they don't listen to it. We can illustrate this point with the story of Lucifer. Lucifer was the most beautiful of the angels, the Archangel who fell from grace and became the devil, suffering separation from God. The same is true of ego or personality; it has a sublime origin which it remembers, and it longs to return to this origin. The ego tries to bring the divine life to earth and actualize it; but it uses ways which don't work. The usual result is a personal life which is an imitation of the true one. The ego can imitate only because, at some level, it knows what the real life would be. It is an imitation only because an original exists. It can't be that we are born to become enlightened and disappear; if we were already pure, why come and suffer, and return to what we were before. What is the point of that?

Many stories and theories attempt to explain why we suffer and have this difficult life. Most of them don't satisfy us. For example, in the story of Adam and Eve, God punishes humanity for not obeying—so why didn't God create us so that we obey? Or there is the idea of karma —there is an accumulation of karma which you need to get rid of to experience your true nature. Where did this karma come from? If your original nature was pure, why do you end up doing things which accumulate karma? Then there are people who say that there is a reason why humanity suffers, but that we are not developed enough to know the reason. Maybe this is true, but how do they know this?

All these questions I'm asking are actually a movement toward being oneself. To be oneself is to question, to ask, "What is this about? I don't want to listen to other people's explanations and stories, I want to know myself. I want to satisfy myself by my own experience, by my own investigation. It doesn't matter what authorities or teachers say if it doesn't make sense in my own experience." The more you question and think for yourself, the more you become yourself. To be oneself means not to be conditioned by others, by the external, not to be an extension of the past, yours or anyone else's past. To be oneself means to be an original.

We are looking at two points of view here, a universal one and a personal one. On one side are the spiritual traditions which speak of a divine, universal life of freedom and enlightenment; on the other side is the rest of humanity who wants a certain kind of life—to be married, find satisfying work, have sex and to fulfill myriad other desires and wishes. Why can't we do both? Why can't we have this personal life and still be free? When you look at your deepest longing, isn't that what you want? You want a normal life, and still to be happy and free; not just free on a mountain retreat, but free in your normal life.

The Hindus say a person should have a family life, and after that they should leave their family and find a teacher or guru to become enlightened. Why leave your life to get enlightened, why not be enlightened in your life? Why do you have to leave your family and your home to become enlightened? What is wrong with all these things? Most people listen to these doctrines and think they should leave it all; they spend the rest of their lives fighting it, and not wanting it to be this way. The reason why people fight it is not just because of their ignorance and ego, but because we know something about our potential. Deep within us is a longing to be a free person, a true person, but still to be a person—to be oneself.

Some teachings about being free from ego might lead you to think that you should get rid of being a person, you should be universal and objective. But, at the deepest level, you want to be a person and be free. Where did you get that idea, that it is possible to be a person and be free at the same time? That longing must originate from somewhere. We know from our method of investigation that if there is a longing then something has been lost. If we have a deep longing, it must be for something real. We might approach the problem wrongly, we might not be clear about what is missing, but the aspiration toward it is real.

How can you be a free person, be yourself, and not be controlled by ego and personality? Is it possible to be oneself without being one's personality? That is the question: if this question is answered then our mystery is solved.

Our work here is to learn how to be free from one's personality by being oneself. The personality as a whole exists because it is taking the place of something real which has been lost. We can feel the potential for this reality in the fact of the existence of its imitator, personality.

The deepest longing in us is to be oneself and to be free at the same time—not to lose oneself completely to be free. We would experience that as a loss. In fact it is not that difficult to lose ourselves, but it is not the most complete fulfillment of human experience. I want to be myself and I want to be free; the freedom is for being myself. As Ramakrishna said, "I don't want to be sugar, I want to taste sugar."

Some say the purpose of human life is to be a channel for the divine energy. How are you different from a tree then, or even a rock? A tree or a rock are channels for the divine energy. It is possible to be a channel, to be a clear, open channel with love and compassion flowing through you. It is a lovely experience but it is not the ultimate reason we are here; it is only transitional. We are not here to be channels, we are here to be.

When you say, "I want to be myself," you usually mean that you want to follow your personality's impulses or express your personality freely. This is as far as you can go in your mind. The mind, at this point, doesn't know it is possible to be oneself without being one's personality. To be yourself still means to be loving when you want to, to be bad when you feel like it, and to have your own way. But when you examine those impulses, those feelings, those dreams that you want to express, you will see that they are determined by your past experience. They are conditioned responses. They are not really you. You might respond to a certain situation or person with anger, for example, and wish to express yourself, be yourself. There is a certain stimulus and the response of anger comes, probably conditioned by your early life with your mother or father. That is not being yourself; that is being an extension of your mother or father. Or you might dream of being a musician; you think that if you are a great musician then you will be being yourself. Perhaps your father loved music and always wanted to be a musician, or even the opposite, perhaps he was a truck driver and didn't care about music and you feel rebellious. You

202 THE FREEDOM TO BE

think, "My father is gross and doesn't care about the finer things in life. I don't want to be like my father, so I'm going to be a composer." You are still an extension of your father, whether you act out his values and wishes or rebel against them. This extension of the past we call personality. When you talk about being yourself you are generally talking about being your personality. As you know, personality is nothing but a product from the past; it is not original or spontaneous. The actions of personality are predetermined by a certain pattern from your childhood which results in mechanical behavior.

To be oneself clearly includes having your own feelings and expressing yourself, but even these are just processes and activities. They may be what is visible, but the central experience, what is germane, is not the expression but the actual experience of Being. To be oneself means to be.

It's true that we need to be free from the personality, just as most traditions say, but it is true because the ego personality is a fraud. The issue is not that personality is bad, but that it is not real, not true. The personality that you usually believe in is not the real you; it's just an imitation. It's an attempt to be you, but the attempt fails.

When did you believe you could be a person? Where did you get that idea? If you are a false person, there must be a real person possible, just as there is imitation gold because there is such a thing as real gold. You can't have a false something if the original which it imitates doesn't exist. Why are people always interested in being original, being themselves, doing their own thing, having their own life, wanting to be autonomous? Can it be that all this drive is simply an illusion, or does it point to something real? If to have a personal life is bad, if pleasure is to be abandoned, if wanting your own home or car means you're selfish, if sharing love with someone is unenlightened, then human life is ridiculous. There must be some hidden truth in all the strivings of mankind.

It is presented in many teachings and traditions that true life begins only in a kind of afterlife, or after enlightenment. This view usually negates the possibility of a true life here and now, or even if it is possible now, this true life would not be life as a person but as a universal experience. What if the free, universal life can happen while being and having oneself? There must be a kernel of truth within all the fairy tales and stories which speak of life being full of magic, beauty, color, charm and festivity. There must be a truth to the beautiful mysteries and to the idea of paradise. One of these stories says that we come from a realm where everyone is royal born, everyone is a king or queen—not a monk or a nun. We are all really of royal descent. It doesn't matter what you do as an occupation in life, you could be a secretary and still know yourself to be a queen. You respect and treat yourself as a queen. Every human being can have this dignity, this freedom. We have a true longing to live as royalty and have dominion over our own lives. It's true that ego longs for those things, and it is also true that desire blocks the experience; but the vision is not false. The vision exists because we are sensing the potential. The understanding of the potential will unify the perspective of the personal with the perspective of the universal. The unification occurs through knowing what it is to be oneself—to be oneself and recognize it. It is a mysterious thing to be oneself in the present, existing, being, instead of reactions from the past. This being is fresh, original every second and in every atom; a being that is itself life, consciousness, existence. This being can never be touched by conditioning, by the past, or by ideas and plans, or by labels such as "spiritual" or "worldly." Not one atom of this being can be touched by the external. I am not a response, an idea, an emotion or a discharge. I exist as me. The mind, the heart, the body, are an external manifestation of me; but I'm the core, the being itself. I am the source and the ground of all of my experience. Only then are my thoughts, actions, and feelings original. Now they have nothing to do with what my mother or father, or even Christ or Buddha, said. To be me does not mean that I am impersonal, universal light. That is a different experience, and that ocean of light, love, bliss is for me. I am its flowering. It is in celebration of me, not the other way around. The pleasure, the joy, the love, the enlightenment are for me—for me as a being. So the being that we truly are is the point of it all, is why there is earth. The reason we are on earth is to be that.

We go through the initiation of life to get to the real thing, not to go back to what we were before. Something in you emerges out of the universal; out of the substance of the universal, a personal arises. I have the universal in me, it is my very soul, my very substance, but I am a person. And that is the miracle. That is the mystery—that the true person includes the universal, includes the divine. The building blocks of the true person are the universal, the divine substance. God creates you fresh in every moment. There is a new birth in that—God gives birth. Without this experience, you will always feel incomplete. It is for the birth and for the growth of this person, the personal being, the personal essence, often referred to as the "Pearl beyond Price," that everything else exists. This is the key, the entry into all the mysteries, and to all the celebrations of existence. To be oneself means to be the synthesis of all that exists as you; to be you. You are the fruit of the universe.

Sufis call the death of the personality "fana," which means extinction. Then they talk about "baqa," which means the remaining after extinction, the existence after death. "Baqa after fana" means "existence in God"; it means to be yourself within the universal. That personal beingness is what is called the Beloved of God in the Koran. In Christianity it is called the Son of God. You cannot be a lover, especially a lover of the divine, unless you are truly yourself. When you are yourself, your personal beingness, then and only then is it possible to treat other people as people, as humans in a personal way. Then they are no longer objects to you.

When you are yourself in this way, it is possible to have personal contact with others. When you are not yourself, when you are the personality of ego, the personality is a barrier between you and the other. Or, if you are the universal aspect, you also cannot make personal contact with someone else. You can envelop them in a universal way, you can be open with them, but that person to person, being to being, heart to heart contact is missing. Some place in the heart of the other person is not touched, and there is no personal meeting. Regardless of how much you love the person, have compassion for him, or want to help him, if you are not personal in your contact, he will not feel met. The personal contact establishes trust.

We need to clarify what we mean by personal. We know that the ego feels personal; the personality is even named after the personal. So how do you tell the true personal from the personality personal? What do we mean when we talk about personal contact? To the personality, it means feelings. "I'm personal because I can tell them all of my feeling. I'm opening my heart to them." That is what is commonly taken to be the personal experience, but this is an imitation just as the whole personality is an imitation.

Personal, for the personality, also means not objective and not universal—it means to be a bounded individual. The personality needs a sense of boundary, of isolation from everything and everyone else. The personal essence doesn't need that sense of isolation or of boundaries. There is no sense of, "I am separate from you." There is no wall between the two of us. The personality has a wall, its edges. So the personality cannot be personal completely; it is like two walls touching. The closest that personality can come to true personal contact is physical contact—two bodies opening to each other, and, actually, in the moment of release, the personality lets go, dissolves for a moment.

Real personal contact occurs when we feel our soul itself is in direct contact with the other person's soul. It is when essence itself is making contact, is itself contactful-ness. I am making contact without completely merging into you or the universal—the contact is immediate and with no boundaries, but still not all one big ocean. The substance of one soul is touching the very substance of another soul, two essences coming together. You are free and spontaneous, not conditioned. You are a fullness, an aliveness, and abundance in being yourself. You being there is a wonderful, pleasurable, sensual fullness. We try to get that full sensuality from the body and through physical contact. That is because we remember, we have a vague memory of what our personal beingness is. Your personal being is like feeling your lover in every cell of your body. You are a voluptuousness, and with that beingness there is joy. To be oneself is true "joi de vivre." Joy is for simply existing; and all value and celebration is of this beingness.

Personal is not in contradistinction to universal; personal is in contradistinction with impersonal. To be personal does not eliminate objectivity; you can be objective without the personality's assumption that objective means cold and unfeeling. When you know yourself this way, you can go through all the levels of spiritual experience—universal included. Then you are truly living your life. You are actually in anything you experience, you are actually doing it. What comes out is a spontaneous response; it has nothing to do with the past. The qualities of essence are within you like your organs are within you—love, compassion, will, the universal, etc.

So you see the mystery is not usually understood because personal is taken to mean personality. The solution is usually thought to be to go to the universal, which is not personal. The personality is in contradiction to the universal. The true personal is not in contradiction to the universal; it is, in fact, a child of the universal, the fruit of the universal.

It is possible to contact your personal aspect, to become aware of who you are, before enlightenment and loss of ego. The moment you know who you are, it becomes easier to know what is not you, what is conditioned, and what is personality. The work is very clear then; there is a guidance. Before that, you don't know where you are going. You don't know what is you and what is not you, what is real, and what is not real—you have no idea. You have only your thoughts and some people's ideas and instructions. But the moment you know who you are, what it is like to be you, once you can recognize this, then you can tell what is you and what is not you.

Some people say that if you really let go of your ego boundaries, then you'll see that you are the universe, and that the stars and galaxies are in you. That is true; however, that is different from the personal. When you are the personal, the universe that you see outside you is completely experienced as inside you, as if you become a miniature universe. When you are truly personal, you are not just merged with the universe, you are a child of the universe. You are the microcosm.

Then you can live on this earth with all the pleasures, with all the festivities, and all the freedom and power—all from the universal, but on earth, as a human being. Then you are everything—a friend, a lover, a warrior. You're the personal and universal with no contradiction. To be oneself is to know oneself from completely original perception. You don't know yourself by contrasting yourself to somebody else; you know yourself without reference to anything else.

We have a longing to be that certain about ourselves. As long as you know yourself as a result of an insight, as a result of comparing yourself to something else, or even fitting your experience with someone else's ideas or experiences, you have no certainty. The longing for this direct certainty, to be oneself, should be the true motivation for the work. You need to make your search as free and as personal as possible. If it is your search and your seeking, it is not according to what anybody says. You can use what any teacher says; learning about their experiences might open parts of you. But ultimately you need to be quite alone. Then your knowledge comes completely from within you, not from any outside pressure. There are always outside pressures and influences; you need to respond to those things from within you and not from a learned pattern. When Buddha says there is no self, you say, "Maybe. Who knows? Let me find out." How can you be certain if you follow blindly? Until I know personally, another's truth is not truth for me, it's an idea or a guiding ideal. I'll try to follow and investigate; I'm open. Since I don't know, I'm open to all ideas, but I follow my own inner flame. Without it, I can't be certain. Somebody could tell me, "You have the Buddha nature." Even if it is validated in books, what difference does it make? It has to be a personal understanding by convincing yourself through your own immediate experience.

Not only is this process the only thing that will work, it is the closest thing to your heart. To be so intimate, so close, so directly in contact with yourself that you are in the atoms of who you are. From within that beingness, that true oneselfness, that intimacy, absolute intimacy, we can live our life and contact others. When we are this intimate, God rejoices for us.

Our life is true to the moment, authentic and completely alone. What we do in our lives, the work we choose, the channels of expression we choose, the way we live, is an external manifestation of that personal beingness. This does not mean you can't be with somebody or have a family. Aloneness means you are yourself and you're not influenced by others. To be completely oneself is to be alone inside; you, with nothing hanging on you, pushing you, pulling you. Then what opens up is a kindness, a warmth, a tenderness, a compassion for oneself.

Who we truly are, our personal beingness is born in a bed of tenderness, kindness, and value. When the true personal essence is born, it is born in a golden cradle covered with a sheet of green.

Student: Would you say that the self destructive things we do are distortions of something true?

A.H. Almaas: Yes. It has to be; there is no other way. Everything that is negative is a distortion of something real. It is a misunderstanding of something true. So I'm saying there is a reason, there is an actual significance to everything. It's not all accidents and mistakes; it is possible to understand every single thought, every single image and to find the truth in it. Each image says something, though it might not be obvious. The thought might be a reaction but if you follow the thought back to the original part, through the defenses, you will see some truth.

S: What is it that gives you direction?

AH: Many things, but one of the main guidelines is to know oneself. The moment you know yourself, you always recognize it. Then, if this is not present you can ask what is stopping it. By understanding what is stopping you, you become yourself again. When all the issues and beliefs and images that block this experience are removed by understanding, then it is not just a state you experience, but a station. A station means that a quality of essence is present whenever there is a need. When you are yourself as a station, you are no longer being guided, you have matured.

S: Could you say something about knowing truth? There are many truths, many truths on different levels, so what is the most direct, efficient process?

AH: You have to be personal in your truth. There might be truth, all kinds of truths in the world, but they are not relevant to you at that moment. You must see what relates to you in that moment, otherwise the question is intellectual, and if it's intellectual you're not going to be able to solve it. But if you take your personal experience at that very moment, you could find the truth right there. It is that personal, free, alone investigation of your moment to moment truth, that will lead you to all truth, all the levels of truth. But if you try to follow what this person says, or that person says, it's hard to know the way. Really it is not possible, because though there may be deep truth in it, it might not be relevant to you at that moment. If it's not relevant there is no need for you to know it then, and it could be an intellectual defense against what you do need at that moment. That's why I emphasize the personal aspect, to be personally involved in your truth. It is your life, it is your experience, it is your every sensation at that moment; it is for you to understand. The truth finally will be revealed in you, to you, if you stay with the moment without prejudice, just exploring the truth. You can't do it from the outside, you need to penetrate and own your own experience.

All truths are relevant for someone. For instance, for someone what is relevant now might be a question of value, not a question of compassion. At the moment they may not care about compassion because they are experiencing a lack of value. Someone might tell them they need to be compassionate and forget about themselves, and they can't. Even if they take it as a working philosophy, they cannot relate to it or contact it. They are in contact with loss of value, and value is a burning issue now, anything else is intellectual.

S: That does something for me. It frees me up from criticism of other people because it's all truth. So there's really no better way because I'm not you and I can't see what way you have to go.

AH: Not everyone can do it, but a guide can and that's what it means to be a teacher. The teacher is the friend who knows and can feel the other person, can know what is her truth. When I'm working with people, often what they need to know is not what I need to know but I am in contact with the aspect that is needed.